MODERN THINKERS
AND
PRESENT PROBLEMS

AN APPROACH TO MODERN PHILOSOPHY
THROUGH ITS HISTORY

BY

EDGAR A. SINGER, Jr., Ph.D.
PROFESSOR OF PHILOSOPHY
IN THE UNIVERSITY OF PENNSYLVANIA

NEW YORK
HENRY HOLT AND COMPANY
1923

PREFACE

THESE papers, which had been written from time to time and for various occasions, have been brought together without any attempt to make them tell a smooth unbroken story, yet not without regard to their connectedness. They have sometimes served me to bring before the mind of youth certain problems on which philosophers have thought again and again. But if they have had any interest for youth, if they are to have any for maturity, it can only be because the names that stand over the chapters might, if moments had names, be those of moments in each man's history.

And as such, unless I have altogether failed to make my characters real, these names will be recognized. Who has not sometime been that Bruno who stepped from his Father's House, where all had revolved so solicitously about himself, to find without the cold stars gazing down on his atomy from their places in endless emptiness?

Who has not come to feel, with Spinoza, those inviolable laws of mechanism which govern the world about him creeping into his own inmost being, threatening there all that he had so simply and yet so dearly clung to as his freedom and autonomy?

How many reflecting in their maturity on the unquestioning faiths of their childhood have thought to bring these to the test of such experience as natural science depends on, only to find, as Hume found, these faiths unconfirmed?

And of those who have lived through this moment of disillusionment, there will always be some who will have come in their own way to the position severe reasoning forced on Kant: The spiritual aspects of reality are not issues of science and intellection, but belong to that other order of truth grasped by the " practical reason."

Others, meanwhile, will have refused to let their speculation go beyond the insight experience yields, and of these some at least will have found that experience holds out nothing hopeful for now or forever. They will have seen with Schopenhauer into the " deep abyss " and found at the bottom of it only this counsel: Not-being is better than being.

Or if perhaps they have for a moment thought, with Nietzsche, that evolutionary science had brought to view a goal that gave heart to the pitiless struggle of life by holding before it the vision of the " far future man," they may in the end have come to see beyond this Superman. But to have seen beyond him nothing but the super-superman is to have seen the goal vanish and the heart lose its hope.

And what then? The pages on " Pragmatism " and on " Progress " may offer suggestions of an answer. They are still historical in their spirit, and like those that had gone before them mean to illustrate, not to demonstrate or affirm. They, too, would stand for moments of any thoughtful life and will have done all they were intended to do if they inform such a life with, and give it a sense of attachment to the world that has gone before and is going on 'round.

But if one would at the outset know something of what the writer suspects to be the outcome of ordered and historically guided reflection on these subjects, let him turn to the closing chapter, if not for encouragement then for warning.

Every one will remember the word to his reader with which Montaigne closes the preface to his Essays. 'Tis but of himself he would write and " it is then no reason thou shouldst employ thy time about so frivolous and vain a subject. Therefore farewell."

I cannot close *my* preface without confessing a misgiving that must have beset everyone who ever wrote of the past: that whereas he set out to lose

PREFACE

himself in history, he may have found in history nothing but himself. But on the bare chance of this having befallen me, I need not say " farewell " beforehand; for well I know no reader will accompany me far through this past save one who finds *him*self there too.

TABLE OF CONTENTS

vii

GIORDANO BRUNO

1548–1600

GIORDANO BRUNO

THE straightest way to the heart of old matters is an old letter. Here is one written on the twenty-third of May, 1592, by a gentleman of Venice to the Father of the Venetian Inquisition.

" Very Reverend Father and Most-to-be-observed Sir:

" I, Gioanni Mocenigo, son of the Clarissimo Messer Marcoantonio, compelled by my conscience and ordered by my confessor, denounce to Your Very Reverend Paternity Giordano Bruno of Nola, whom I have heard say on various occasions when he was conversing with me in my own house, that Catholics do but blaspheme when they hold the Bread to be transubstantiated into the Flesh; that he is against the Mass; that no religion satisfies him; that Christ was a charlatan who, since he resorted to tricks to fool people, might well enough have foreseen that he would die a criminal's death; that there is no distinction of Persons in God; . . . that the world is eternal and that there are an infinite number of worlds, and that God is continually making an infinity of them because He wants as many as He can

3

have; that Christ performed specious miracles; that he was a magician and the apostles were magicians too." . . .

The letter runs on in breathless denunciation, but already one begins to make out the image of Bruno reflected in the average mind of his time. The limited intelligence of Mocenigo has honestly misunderstood some of Bruno's utterances, his malice has distorted others; but the perversity of the whole is not due to these faults of detail. Lost in this jumble of stock heresies lies hidden a great idea, the greatest perhaps that has ever been contributed by a single mind to the cause of our science. " And he says the world is eternal and that there are an infinity of worlds." This sentence has brought the old world to an end, has shattered the heavens under which Christendom was then living, yet it falls on the ear of its time with no more meaning or portent than a doubt respecting the doctrine of transsubstantiation or the authenticity of miracles. Bruno, throughout the course of his driven life and up to the moment of his tragic death, knew most forms of martyrdom. He bore none of these meekly, for his was a lusty soul that did not love to suffer. But neither the hatred nor the cruelty of his world seems to have hurt him so to the quick as did its stupidity. Doubt him and hate if you will; but value him you

4

must! He was master of a great idea and unacquainted with modesty.

Meanwhile Mocenigo has more to say of this sinner: " He has expressed the intention of making himself the founder of a new sect under the name of the new philosophy. He has said that the Virgin could not have brought a child into the world, and that our Catholic faith is full of blasphemies against the majesty of God; that it would be better to suppress the largesses of wrangling friars because they befoul the world; that they are all asses and that our common opinions are the teaching of asses; that we have no proof that our faith has merit with God; that the simple rule of not doing unto others what we would not have done unto us is sufficient for right living.". . . Perhaps I may stop here. Evidently one who could be guilty of all these follies would be ingenious in inventing others, and Mocenigo's letter may run endlessly on.

While this letter was writing, Bruno lay locked in a room of Mocenigo's house. " I had thought to learn from him," Mocenigo explains, " not knowing him to be the wicked man he is, and having noted all these things to lay before your Very Reverend Paternity, and fearing that he would take his departure as he said he wished to do, I have locked him in a room at your disposal. As I think him possessed of the devil, I hope you will decide quickly what is to be done with him. . . ."

It has sometimes been wondered how Bruno came to accept the invitation of Mocenigo to take up his residence in Venice. Italy was for him a place of such peril that it seems incredible he should have ventured to set foot in it. " Tell me one thing more," concludes a letter written in this same year 1592 by a gentleman of Bologna to a friend in Padua, " tell me one thing more. Giordano Bruno, whom you knew at Wittenberg, the Nolan, is said to be living among you just now at Padua. Is it really so? What sort of man is this that he dares to enter Italy, which he left in exile as he himself used to confess? I wonder, I wonder. I cannot yet believe the rumor, although I have it on good authority. You shall tell me whether it is true." And history has wondered all the more seeing that Bruno himself had long before prophesied the result. " Torches," he had written, " fifty or a hundred, will not fail me though the march be at noonday should it be my fate to die in a Catholic country."

So far as documents furnish any answer to this question, it lies suggested in a second letter written by Mocenigo to the Holy Inquisition two days after the denunciation. " In the course of the day that I kept Giordano Bruno locked up, I asked him whether the things that he would not teach me, as he promised to do in return for the many kindnesses I had done him and the many gifts that I had given him, whether he would not consent to teach me them if I abstained from denouncing him for all the criminal things he had uttered to me against our Lord Jesus Christ and against the Holy Catholic Church. He answered that he did not fear the Inquisition, for he had harmed no one by living in his own way, and moreover he could not recall having said anything sinful, but that if he had said such things he had said them only to me, and he need not fear that I would do him harm in the way I suggested." Those who can may believe that Bruno is here telling the truth about himself. Those who can may believe that he who eight years before and at a safe distance from Italy had so clearly seen the torches that awaited him there, had since grown blind to them or indifferent.

The next document of the trial is brief enough. Under date of the following day — that is, Tuesday, the twenty-sixth of May — is found this entry: " Clarissimo Dom Aloysius Fuscari presiding. Presented himself Dom Matheus de Avantio, Captain of the Constabulary, and reported as follows: Sabbath at three o'clock of the night,[1] I arrested

---

[1] This would be Saturday afternoon.

Giordano Bruno of Nola, whom I found in a house over against Saint Samuels, in which dwells the Clarissimo Ser Gioanni Mocenigo, and I have imprisoned him in the Prisons of the Holy Office, and this I have done by order of this Holy Tribunal."

The doors of the prison closing on Bruno bring to an end the story of his life, but from behind these doors there come to us fragments of the story itself as Bruno retells it to his judges. For on the very day of his arrest he is examined by a tribunal composed of the Apostolic Nuncio, the Patriarch of Venice, the Very Reverend Father Inquisitor. Before these, as the clerk of the tribunal records it, was brought a certain man of ordinary height with a chestnut beard, who, when he had been admonished to speak the truth, and before any question could be put to him, burst out of his own accord: " I will tell the truth. Several times have I been threatened with being brought before this Holy Office, but I have always taken the threat for a joke, because I am ever ready to give account of myself." Whereupon he tells how, having found himself at Frankfurt the previous year, he received there two letters from Gioanni Mocenigo, inviting him to come to Venice to instruct Mocenigo in the art of memory and the art of invention, for which this Venetian gentleman had promised to pay him well and treat him in a way that should content him. And so Bruno had come to Venice seven or eight months before, living first in lodgings, then for a brief space in Padua, until some two months prior to his arrest he had taken up his residence in Mocenigo's own house. We already know how, " compelled by his conscience and ordered by his confessor," Mocenigo finally disposed of his guest.

Then Bruno questioned by the tribunal, laid before it a formal account of his life. " My name is Giordano Bruno, of the family of the Bruni, of the city of Nola, twelve miles from Naples. In this place I was born and raised, and my profession was and is letters and the sciences. My father was named Gioanni, and my mother Fraulissa Savolina, and my father's calling was that of a soldier. He is dead since, and my mother too.

" I am about forty-four years of age, and I was born, so far as I have heard from my people, in the year 1548. I remained in Naples learning the humanities, logic, and dialectics until fourteen years of age . . . and then I took the habit of Saint Dominic in the monastery or convent of Saint Dominic in Naples, and was invested by a Padre who was then prior of that convent, called Maestro Ambrosio Pasqua. When the year of probation was passed, I was admitted by him to profession, which was

9

solemnly made in the same convent. . . . Later I was promoted to holy orders and at the usual season to the priesthood. I sang my first mass in Campagnia, a city of the same state at a distance from Naples, residing the while in a convent of the order, the San Bartholomeo, and continued in the religious habit of Saint Dominic, celebrating masses and the divine offices, obedient to the superior of the Order and to the priors of the monasteries and convents where I was stationed until 1576. . . ."

I have not wanted to interrupt Bruno, nor to hurry him in his story, tedious as it is in the telling. Little event after little event of his secular and of his religious life befalls with the trivial monotony of dropping rain. But is it not just so that these little events and endless others like them must have fallen on the soul of the living Bruno, soaking in, soaking in, unnoticed as rain, until his very humors ran with their humor? Now their humor was the spirit of the old world, the spirit of his Father's House. Would it not be curious if, having pulled down this ridiculous old dwelling and in the very act of dancing among its ruins, Bruno should suddenly come to see that it was the only house his soul, being such a soul as it was, could dwell in? If something of this kind did not happen at a moment of his life we are fast approaching, then only the gods know what did happen. But I am anticipating, or rather laying up reflections against our hour of need. For the moment we have no more than come to the day in Bruno's life when he stepped out of his Father's House to make his way *ins Freie hinaus*.

Fifty years ago, before Berti had unearthed the documents of this trial, it was difficult to trace the life of Bruno. Since then it has become well-nigh impossible. Documents are a great embarrassment to the conscientious historian. They are there, these documents, and have to be put in the text; the truth about the case must be relegated to the foot-notes. Now the text runs in this wise: " In 1576 . . . I was in Rome at the Convent of Minerva, obedient to the orders of Maestro Sisto de Luca, Procurator of the Order. Thither I had gone to present myself because at Naples two processes had been instituted against me, the first for having given away certain images of the saints and retaining only a crucifix, it being thought that this showed a lack of respect for the images of the saints; and the other for having said to a novice who was reading a story of the Seven Beatitudes in verse, What did he think he was doing with a book like that? — why didn't he throw it away and read rather some other book, as the lives of the Holy Fathers? This process was renewed at

reason imprisoned within the confines of imaginary heavens. . . . We know that there is but one heaven, one immense ether, where magnificent fires maintain their proper distances by reason of that eternal life in which they have part. These flaming bodies are the ambassadors which announce the excellence of God's glory and majesty."

This is indeed the voice of an Awakener. But, alas for awakeners! the vision of the morning is never fair to those just shaken out of their dreams. In an introductory letter to the last of the dialogues we catch an echo of the sleeper's complaint: " If I shoved a plow, if I kept a flock, if I cultivated a garden, if I mended old clothes, no one would notice me, few would consider me, not many would find fault with me, and I could easily please everybody. But for having been studious of the field of nature, solicitous for the pasture of the soul, enamored of the cultivation of the mind, a very Daedalus fashioning raiment for the intellect, every passer-by threatens me, every one who sees me attacks me, who comes upon me rends me, who lays hold on me devours. It is not one, it is not a few; it is many, it is almost all. If you would know why this is, I will tell you the reason of it — I despise the crowd, I hate the mob, the multitude contents me not. One thing I love, one thing for whose sake I am free in bondage, content in pain, rich in poverty, alive in very death. One thing for whose sake I envy not those who are slaves in their liberty, troubled in their pleasure, poor in their riches, dead in their life. Their body is the chain that binds them, in their mind is the hell that tortures them, in their spirit the falsehood that makes them sick, in their soul the lethargy that kills. Not theirs the greatness of mind which frees, the breadth of view which ennobles. Not theirs the splendor which illumines, nor the science which gives life." It is a brave, even an over-brave flourish with which Bruno ends this proemial epistle: " And so the gods deliver me from all those who unjustly hate me, and my God be always propitious unto me! . . . The stars let my sowing fit the field and the field my sowing, that the world be made content with the useful and glorious fruits of my labors! . . . And if I err, I truly do not believe myself to err; whether speaking or writing, I do not dispute for the love of victory. . . . For love of true wisdom and desire for true insight I exhaust, I crucify, I torture myself. . . ."

Brave is the flourish, how over-brave we realize with unexpected intensity as we follow this solemn trial to its last scene. Having recounted the episodes of his life, Bruno proceeds to the explanation and

ships to receive punishment for the saving of my soul. My soul cannot express the depth of its contrition for my fault." And falling on his knees, he said, " I humbly ask pardon of the Lord God and of Your Most Illustrious Lordships for all the errors which I have committed and which I now stand ready to expiate in such wise as your wisdom may think proper and judge expedient for my soul. And moreover, I beg that you give me a punishment which shall exceed in severity rather than set any public example which may throw dishonor on the sacred religious habit I have worn. And if by God's mercy and the mercy of Your Most Illustrious Lordships, life shall be spared me, I promise to make such notable reform of my life as shall pay for the scandal I have given with equal and greater edification."

In this unhappy posture I leave Bruno the man to take up the story of his great idea. We shall see him once more indeed, at the moment when, eight years later, he calmly dies for the idea he now so abjectly abandons; but no understanding of the alternating enthusiasm and despair that filled this life can afford to neglect the qualities of the gospel it stood for, forsook, then died for in the end.

Like all very great ideas, this one is of the simplest. It begins with the observation that the flame of a candle grows bigger as we approach it, smaller as we recede from it. Nothing very new in this, you say, nor very imposing. No, it is the next step that was so new in Bruno's day, and of such tremendous destructive and creative power. Yet it is just as simple as the first. What is true of a candle flame must be true of a sun and of a star. Is it not indeed simple? Yes, but in all the long while the world had lasted it had occurred to no one before Bruno to seize upon this simple idea and to follow whither it led. It led far, wonderfully far. It led Bruno to journey in imagination out and out toward those most distant stars that were then called fixed, and were indeed supposed to be fixed in one great sphere that enclosed all things, beyond which was nothing, and not even nothing, for there was no beyond; space ended where matter ended, at the walls of the world. But Bruno as he journeyed saw this great sun of ours growing smaller and smaller as he receded from it, and yonder star growing larger and larger as he approached it, until the most wonderful thing happened. The sun began to look more and more like a star, and the star more and more like a sun. There was now no escaping the conclusion — the stars that had been called fixed are other suns, our sun but a near-lying star.

neyings to men, he came to perceive, as these men at once perceived, that his new vision was not all made of beauty? Is there not in this infinite cosmos that which may depress and even terrify?

In his " Garden of Epicurus," Anatole France has put the two worlds side by side. One has only to do this to feel that Bruno, who at first held out his hands to the new vision, may afterwards have snatched them back again to shut it out.

" We have some trouble," says France, " in imagining the state of mind of a man in olden times who firmly believed that the Earth was the center of the Universe, and that all the stars turned round it. He felt under his feet damned souls writhing in flames, and perhaps he had seen with his own eyes, and smelled with his own nostrils the sulphurous fumes of Hell escaping from some fissures in the rocks. Lifting his head he contemplated the spheres, . . . those bearing the Moon, Mercury, Venus — the one that Dante visited on Good Friday of the year 1300 — the Sun, Mars, Jupiter, Saturn, then the incorruptible firmament from which the stars were suspended like lamps. Beyond, his mind's eye discerned the Ninth Heaven to which the saints were rapt, the Primum Mobile or Crystalline; and finally Empyrion, dwelling of the blessed, toward which, he firmly hoped, two angels robed in white would

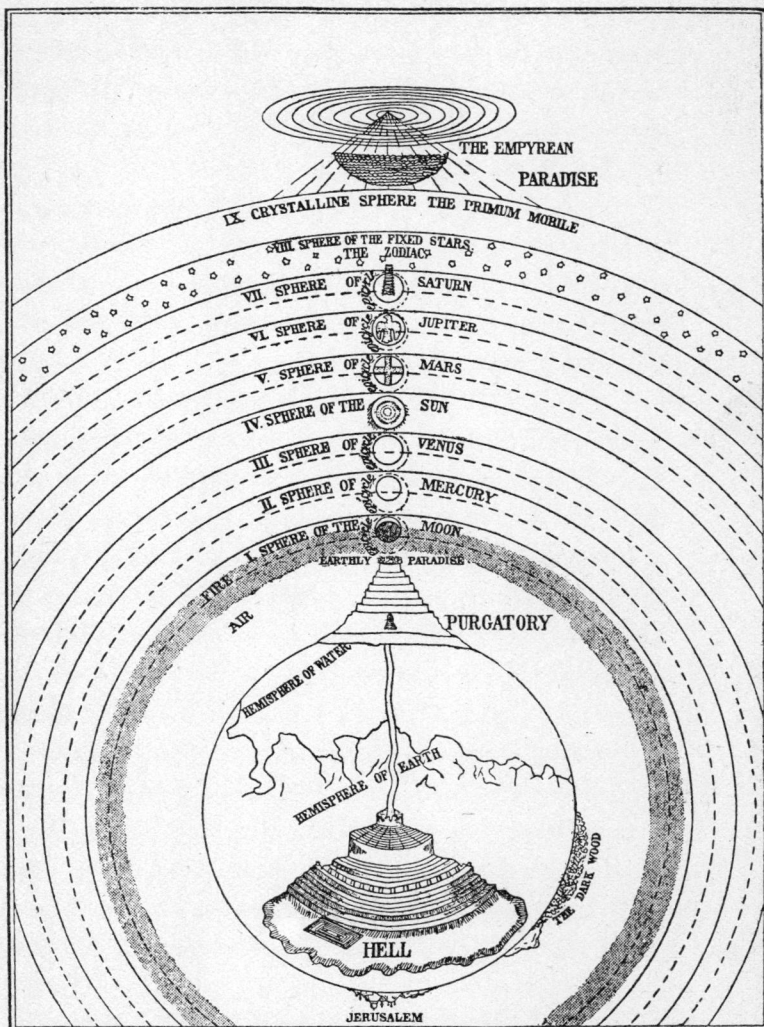

DANTE'S CONCEPTION OF THE UNIVERSE

(From Hearnshaw's *Mediæval Contributions to Modern Civilization*.)

bear away, as it were a little child, his soul washed in baptism and perfumed with the oil of the last sacraments. In those days God had no other children than man, and all his creation was ordered in a fashion at once childlike and poetic like an immense cathedral. Thus imagined, the universe was so simple that it was represented in its entirety with its true figure and motions in certain great clocks run by machinery and appropriately painted."

But now! " We are done with the spheres and the planets under which one was born lucky or unlucky, jovial or saturnine. The solid vault of the firmament is shattered. Our eye and our thought plunge into infinite abysses of heaven. Beyond the planets we discover no longer the Empyrion of the elect and of the angels, but a hundred millions of rolling suns escorted by their cortège of obscure satellites invisible to us. In the midst of this infinity of worlds our own Sun is but a bubble of gas and our Earth but a fleck of mud."

The contrast speaks for itself and needs no comment. It is enough to point out the effect it must have had upon the ethical and religious notions of him who first realized it. What in such a world are we to make of the central episode of Christianity? Bruno's imagination that had swept through space and sped by the stars had found these worlds inhabited by beings " perhaps better, perhaps worse than we are." If there was no evidence that these dwellers in distant solar systems were so much better than we as to need no saving, neither was there any evidence that they were so much worse as to deserve none. We were no longer the only children of God. What then? Are we to suppose that the drama of Redemption is being enacted over and over again throughout the infinity of worlds? Is the Son of God being sacrificed over and over again for the sake of His other children? Is He at this moment perhaps redeeming with His life the dwellers on some star in the night yonder?

But destruction did not stop here. Not only the gentler aspects which Christianity had given to the sterner religion of pagandom were threatened. That older religion itself, with its well-thought-out theory of the relation between God and man, must either be rejected or remodeled. For Aristotle as well as for Aquinas, God and man had formed the real plot of the universe. God, revealing himself most clearly in the turning of the enclosing heaven, set thereby the rest of nature in motion and stirred things down to their very center. So that in the region of earth, water, air and fire there came to be composed bodies mixed of all these. They were the living beings we know, which, holding their ingredients in proper proportion for a while, fell apart again and passed away.

These living beings differed in power. As we pass from the vegetable through the animal to the human they show themselves increasingly able to control the matter in which and of which they are. Highest of all is the human male. It is for the sake of producing him that the mechanism which fills the region between Heaven and Earth exists and is operated. One might almost say that Nature is God's workshop for producing man. But why should God be thus interested in producing this particular kind of animal? Aristotle's answer comes less clearly than one could wish, yet it comes. It is because man differs from the animals not only in degree but in kind. He is not altogether animal. In his superior body there is contained a soul which is not only of God's making, but of God's very substance. That is why man alone can know God. It is as though God needed to be known, recognized, reflected as in a mirror. As for man, he is a bit of divinity momentarily estranged from his home and dwelling, but with the privilege of returning thither can he but free his soul from earthly and sensuous entanglements and interest himself in knowing his Father which is in Heaven.

And now that Bruno has destroyed this difference

between Heaven and Earth, has he not destroyed along with it the distinction between God and man? Has not his infinite homogenous world left man a mere mite shivering on his fleck of mud as it rolls around its bubble of gas? Man is no longer the center of interest; he no longer plays an important part in any thinkable plot. " Man is no more than an ant in the presence of the infinite," cries Bruno. " A star is no more than a man."

We can understand that Bruno's awakening, with however great an enthusiasm it may have been heralded, can be no pleasant awakening for the sleeper. The world of his dreams was infinitely fairer and warmer than that reality to whose garish light his eyes have been opened. It cannot be expected that the awakened should feel any gratitude, and he did not. But what is less obvious is the matter of Bruno's own feeling as the consequences of his new idea gradually unfold themselves to him. Can that first enthusiasm be sustained to the end, or must he too shrink before the fuller vision of what he has done?

If we were to classify men in terms of their reactions to new ideas, I think we should all hit upon these three types. Let me call the first the radical. He is easy to initiate into a new truth, bold to accept it at all costs, loses at once all perspective and sees in the past only a bundle of errors without beauty and with no other interest than to furnish matter for jest. And then there is the conservative. The hold that the past has on such a mind is sometimes enormous. He is capable of clinging to it at the expense of all the rest of his science and experience. If it has enthralled his heart and imagination, he falls into a mood which the Renaissance called the acceptance of " two-fold truth." He believes against all evidence. He believes as Tertullian had it, just because the thing is absurd. He insists with Pascal, that the heart has its reasons which the reason cannot understand. He is a creature of faiths and of mysticisms. Finally there is the philosopher, the only one of the three completely made for unhappiness. He gets no thrill from novelty. He has followed human thought through too many revolutions to expect the most violent of cataclysms to change things much. He struggles to keep his perspective as he would keep his reason, and the views of older humanity do not lose their beauty because their expression has been proved wrong. Required to readjust his thought of yesterday to the new fact of today, he undertakes the task cheerfully enough as part of the day's work. That is what yesterdays, todays, and if it may be, tomorrows are given to him for.

He measures his success by the extent to which he can mold new thought to the satisfaction of old desire, to old desire newly instructed.

And Bruno — to which of these classes does he belong? Is he the radical who would light-heartedly take his place on the fleck of mud and watch it roll around its bubble of gas, while he laughs at his neighbors, who in the face of such a universe charm themselves into a continued faith that they are somehow divine souls in whom a God of Heaven is interested? Or will he, on the other hand, become one of those thus held by the past? Will the awakener, now himself fully awakened, try to snatch at the fading dream and somehow manage to keep his faith in what he knows can't be true? Or will he set laboriously to work, as a philosopher should, to find that interpretation of the new facts which lies closest to the meaning, though it may differ from the verbal expression of world-old desires and longings?

Alas! if Bruno would but make up his mind to be any one of these three, the task of his biographer would be easy. But the real Bruno, the Bruno who mocked, who thought, who recanted, and who died, was not a type. He was a man, and as he was the most human of men, he gathered the greatest possible number of inconsistencies to his heart. Yes, he was a radical who mocked and jeered. Yes, he was a philosopher who labored and thought. And yes, finally, he was a mystic who could hold as a splendid if inexplicable possession of his faith, all the things his reason showed to be impossible. I have shown you Bruno's mockery reflected in the somewhat muddy and turbid medium of Mocenigo's denunciation. I have shown you Bruno the mystic, kneeling before the Inquisition, completely abandoning the great idea. It remains for me to show Bruno the philosopher, Bruno the Pantheist, Bruno the unacknowledged inspiration of much that is recognized as great in Spinoza and Leibnitz, the acknowledged and highly honored forerunner of much we take to be greatest in the German Idealism that centers about 1800.

We left the great idea at the moment, when, having pierced the heavens, it had come to realize the consequences of its act. The gentle meaning of Christ, the sterner pagan wisdom of God and man had been lost in an infinity that knew no enclosing heaven, in a dreary waste of sameness that knew no distinction, not even that between man and God. Bruno the philosopher was not one to let this work of scientific devastation go on unchallenged. What if there were a God who could dwell just as clearly in a heaven that was everywhere as in a Heaven that was above? What if man could have an interest for and could serve this God, not because he was different in kind from the ant, but because he was, or rather in proportion as he was, different in degree? Does not the life that quickens an animate thing pervade that thing? Is it not the same life which in me beckons with my finger, beats with my heart, thinks with my brain? What then if this infinite world of ours were one great living thing made up of other living things, as our body is made up of finger, and heart, and brain, each of which in doing its own work does consciously or unconsciously the work of the whole? " Natura est Deus in rebus." This is one of the phrases Bruno found in trying to express his philosophy. Nature is God in things, or let us put it — God is the life; suns and planets, men and ants, falling rain and mounting mist are but the gestures of this life. Each thinks it does what it does for its own sake, but those who think clearest realize that the joy of their doing as well as the solace of their undoing is the part they play in working out the ideal of the whole. " And He lives in me as I live in my hand " — the phrase is Von Hofmannsthal's, the thought is Bruno's, and it is the whole thought of Bruno the Pantheist.

The end of this life is told in a letter written by

one Gaspard Schopp (a converted Lutheran) to his friend Rittershausen, rector of the University of Altdorf:

"If I write to you now, it is because this very day Giordano Bruno was publicly burned for heresy in the Field of Flowers in front of the theater of Pompey. . . . If you were in Rome, you would learn from each and every Italian that a Lutheran was burned, and so you would be not a little strengthened in your opinion of our savage hatred. But you must know, my Rittershausen, that our Italians do not draw a sharp line between heretics and heretics, nor do they know fine distinctions, but if any one is a heretic they take him for a Lutheran, in which simplicity I pray that God may continue them. . . .

"Now Bruno was that Nolan . . . a professed Dominican who some twenty-three years agone began to doubt of Transubstantiation . . . then forthright to deny it, and likewise the virginity of the Blessed Mary. He migrated to Geneva, . . . whence, not approving himself altogether sound in his Calvinism (than which, nevertheless, nothing leads straighter to atheism), he was driven to Lyons, whence to Toulouse, from whence he passed on to Paris, where he was a professor, but extraordinarius, as he found that the professor ordinarius was obliged to attend Mass. Thence to London, where he published a little book called the 'Beast Triumphant,' meaning thereby the Pope, whom your party is wont to honor with the name of beast.[1] From here to Wittenberg, where, if I am not mistaken, he lectured publicly for two years. Having gone on to Prague, he published there the works, 'On the Boundless,' 'On the Innumerable Worlds,' and yet one other, 'On the Shadows of Ideas,' in which he taught horrible and moreover most absurd things, as that there are innumerable worlds, that the soul passes from one body into another, . . . that magic is a good thing and permissible, the Holy Spirit is nothing but the soul of the world, and that this was what Moses meant when he wrote, 'The spirit of God moved on the face of the waters,' that the world is eternal. . . . In a word, whatever is asserted by the Pagan philosophers, whatever by our older or newer heretics he (Bruno) maintained.

"From Prague he went on to Brunswick and Helmstadt, and there for a time is said to have taught. Then to Frankfurt for the publishing of certain books, and later fell into the hands of the Inquisition at Venice, whence when they had had enough of him, he was sent to Rome. Frequently examined by the Holy Office . . . of the Inqui-

---

[1] A curious ignorance of the content of the " Spaccio! " There are numerous other faults of detail in this account.

sition, convicted by the highest theologians, he now besought eighty days that he might consider, now promised recantation, now defended his point anew, now obtained another eighty days; but was really doing nothing but make a fool of the Pontiff and the Inquisition.

" So that, nearly eight years after he had come before the Inquisition here, on the ninth of February in the Palace of the Grand Inquisitor, there being present the Most Illustrious Cardinals of the Holy Office of the Inquisition, . . . theologians of counsel, and the secular magistrate, governor of the city, Bruno was brought in, and on bended knees heard sentence pronounced against him. And it was in this way: the story of his life was told, of his studies and teachings, and with what diligence and fraternal admonishment the Inquisition had sought to effect his conversion, and what obduracy and impiety he had shown. Then they defrocked him, as we say, and straightway excommunicated him and handed him over to the secular arm to be punished, asking that this be done with clemency and without the shedding of blood.

" While this was passing he answered nothing, except this word: ' In greater fear, perhaps, do you impose sentence upon me than I do receive it.' So, taken away to prison by the governor's lictors, he was allowed a fortnight in case he should wish to recant his errors; but in vain. Today he was led to the stake. When the image of our Saviour on the Cross was shown to him as he was about to die, he turned away his head and sullenly rejected it. In great misery he thus died, and is gone, I think, to tell in those other worlds of his imagining after what manner the men of Rome are wont to treat impious blasphemers. . . ."

Surely, he came to that other world of his imagining. It is our world and he dwells among us. Little does he remember of the men of Rome, of their Illustrious Lordships of Venice, of all the toil and travail of that old life of his — hardly enough to fill an idle hour in the telling. But we know him easily for the unchanged soul he was. He is that one who came to us of a day and opened our eyes to new and troubling visions. " Now you are free," he said, " be glad! " He is that same one who stole back another day and whispered, " But you are afraid! Remember your Father's House, how safe it was and warm." He may be there to close the eyes that have seen enough, with what counsel then, who can tell? But once he was fond of saying, " Not only he who wins deserves the laurels; but also he who dies no coward."

II

BENEDICT DE SPINOZA
1632–1677

BENEDICT DE SPINOZA

" ALL things excellent are as difficult as they are rare." These words which bring to a close Spinoza's masterpiece " Ethics, after the manner of Geometry," sum up the experience of a life as rare as it was difficult.

But then, the things that make life difficult are so much a question of the nature that accepts or invites them! We may be sure that few, brought to the lap of Lachesis, would have the courage to pick therefrom Spinoza's lot. To be born of exiled Jews, to be cast off by family and race as an offender against holy traditions, to live then in loneliness among Christians whose faith one does not accept, to die by inches at the age of forty-five, — even as lives go this would hardly be called an easy one. How seriously then must we take the sustaining power of a philosophy which enabled Spinoza, partly accepting, partly inviting his destiny, to lend it an aspect of calm beauty that touches our wonder!

One is tempted to recall the unhappy Bruno; without, tossed and hunted; within, torn by a conflict between a new science at once grand and desolate, and a memory of things lovable but untrue. In him a lofty philosophy was to have quieted this struggle and consoled this isolation but did not, unless indeed it did at that last moment when he stood at his stake in the Field of Flowers.

There is much likeness but an all-important difference between Bruno and Spinoza, whose names a curious fate linked together first in general condemnation, then in general praise. The two were alike in this, that if anything more lonely can be conceived than the fugitive existence of Bruno, it is the monk-like reclusion of Spinoza; if anything more desolate than the infinite wind-swept universe of Bruno, it is this same universe bereft of the quivering life and all-inspiring purpose that Bruno found in it, this world left on our hands a rolling mechanism fatal and purposeless. But the difference is profound. The philosophy, yes, one may boldly say the religion of Spinoza, sustained him from day to day, from hour to hour. Bruno's was rather the poet's vision, vivid enough while it lasted, but dispelled by the shock of reality to return only at such moments as that in which his life went out. Is it in the power of a thought, is it in the temperament of a man that this difference lies explained?

BENEDICT DE SPINOZA

Spinoza's thought, whatever its worth, owned a distinguished lineage. When in 1658 he was excommunicated by the Jews at Amsterdam, he turned with eager curiosity to the learning if not to the faith of the Christians. In particular the Dutch physician, Francis Van den Ende, himself a freethinker, became his teacher and friend. From him Spinoza acquired his knowledge of Latin and German, by him was initiated into the sciences and introduced to the works of Giordano Bruno and of one other destined to play a determining part in his thought, René Descartes — " the father of modern philosophy " as he is sometimes called.

Descartes, whose life overlaps that of Bruno at the one end and of Spinoza at the other, is founder of the school of thought the historian calls Rationalistic. Now a rationalist is obviously enough one who is bent on following his reason, but reason as opposed to what? We think first of reason as opposed to authority and revelation; but although rationalism came inevitably to discard these sources of belief — had already discarded them in the thought of our very Spinoza — the father of rationalism had left some room for both; partly because it might furnish a convenient refuge if the official church with which he desired to live in comfortable relation should press him; partly because

BENEDICT DE SPINOZA

I do not propose to develop here the tortured processes of reasoning by which the rationalists were wont to convince themselves that *what* God is and *that* He is, were no mere questions of experience. It seemed to them as though the very meaning of God assured his existence. But I question if in the end any of our day would be strongly convinced by their argument about it. The whole matter is of the less importance that Spinoza's results in the domain of ethics are not so dependent on his method but that one may readily reword the problem of 17th century rationalism in the language of modern science.

Nevertheless it is in the first instance devotion to the method he had received from Descartes that requires Spinoza to differ with his master on two points of the greatest importance to the sequel. This God, this " all-perfect being " as the rationalists commonly defined Him, plays a rather capricious part in Descartes' thinking. He is represented as the Creator of the physical universe, and in this act of creation as quite arbitrarily choosing this sort of a world rather than another, a world working out a destiny that is not chosen because it is good but is good because it is chosen of *God*. For the rest, what this end may be is beyond the ken of human reason, and after having done homage to the divine purpose Descartes feels at liberty to confine his attention to studying the mechanism and reconstructing the history of nature as we find it.

Here one can imagine Spinoza exclaiming " What! You would follow the guidance of the geometers, deducing all truth from the axiom of God's existence, and you leave it to God to decide what shall and what shall not follow from his nature! " Do then the axioms of geometry select the theorems they shall establish, accepting some and rejecting others for a motive whether good or bad? No, says Spinoza, God has neither intellect nor will: facts and laws follow from His nature as the properties of a triangle from its definition.

The other element of caprice in Descartes' final picture of the world is just *man*. He alone of all things occupying a place in God's universe is not subjected to mechanical law. But how, Spinoza may well ask, can we conceive ourselves to be following the lead of mathematicians if we violate the first principles of their science? Does the geometry of a triangle depend upon the place in which the triangle finds itself? How then can the laws of the behavior of bodies depend upon these bodies being in or out of the human machine? The human body must be determined by the same laws of physics that govern all extended things. " And as for the mind," Spinoza adds, " the order and connection of its ideas

tage, as for example, the eyes for seeing, the teeth for chewing, plants and animals for food, the sun for giving light, and so on, this has led them to regard all things in nature as means to their advantage. And knowing these means to have been discovered, not provided by themselves, they have made this a reason for believing that there is some one else who has provided them for their use. But as they had never had any information concerning the character of this being, they had to judge it from their own. Hence, they maintained that the gods direct all things with a view to man's advantage, to lay men under obligation to themselves, and to be held in the highest honor; whence it has come to pass that each one has thought out for himself, according to his disposition, a different way of worshipping God, that God might love him above others, and direct all nature to the service of his . . . desire. But while they sought to show that nature does nothing uselessly (in other words nothing that is not to man's advantage) they seem to have shown only that nature and gods and men are all equally mad."

And Spinoza seizes the opportunity to pay tribute to a respectable, well-worn theology:

" Just see how far the thing has been carried! Among all useful things in nature they could not help finding a few harmful things, as tempests, earthquakes, diseases, etc. They maintained that these occurred because the gods were angry on account of injuries done them by men or on account of faults committed in their worship. And although experience daily contradicted this and showed by an infinity of instances that good and evil fall to the lot of the pious and of the impious indifferently, that did not make them abandon their inveterate prejudice. They found it easier to class these facts with other unknown things whose use they could not name and thus to retain their present and innate condition of ignorance, than to destroy the whole fabric of their reasoning and think out a new one. Hence they assumed that the judgment of the gods very far surpasses man's power of comprehension." This in itself, Spinoza concludes, would have been sufficient to hide the truth forever from mankind had not science, which looks into the why and not the wherefore of things, shown men a different standard of truth.

The second paragraph in which he fulfils his promise to show the folly of the popular belief in a providence is pervaded by a dry humor:

" I must not overlook the fact that the adherents of this doctrine who have chosen to display their ingenuity in assigning final causes to things, have employed in support of their doctrine a new form of

thermore we should fail to see how he could have called his great work an " ethics," inasmuch as it is hardly to be understood how in a world where every act of the body is necessitated by eternal laws of physics, every thought of the mind by equally rigid laws of psychology, there could be such a thing as a good or bad act, a good or bad thought. Where there is no freedom, how can there be right and wrong, worth and unworthiness?

And yet we shall find that into this hard inhospitable world-picture, Spinoza has set a theory of life that not only recognizes and defines the difference between the good and the bad, but culminates in a phrase whose religious feeling is unmistakable: Virtue is knowledge; the only knowledge is to know God; to know God is to love him. If one grasp this part of his philosophy, one will understand how it came about that him whom the eighteenth century called atheist, the nineteenth remembered as a *Gottrunkener Mensch* — a God-intoxicated man.

It would be too much to attempt to follow the technical expression that Spinoza gives to his thought. Every word is heavy with the burden of long centuries of scholasticism. But I think it is not impossible to put oneself in possession of one principal idea on which the rest follows, not without jolt, yet with a fair degree of ease.

Let us then put the problem clearly before us. Suppose Nature, including the incident of human life, were one great machine without purpose in the whole, without freedom in the detail, how would it be possible to regard any part of nature, a given man for example, as either good or bad? If this man lives as he must, what use, nay what meaning in advising him how he *ought* to live?

Spinoza's answer involves this fundamental point. There are some machines that exist for a purpose. We may, if we choose, regard it as *the nature* of such a machine to accomplish this purpose. In proportion as it accomplishes it we call it good; in proportion as it fails we call it bad. Thus a clock is mechanical enough, a matter of cogwheels and springs, but that is not *the nature* of a clock, for we can recognize such an implement without knowing anything about these same cogwheels and springs, if only we know that the thing keeps time. As it keeps accurate time we call it a good clock, and as it loses or gains we call it a bad one. It is true that we do not exactly blame the clock if it goes wrong; we rather blame the clock-maker. But there is no reason why we should cease to blame the clock-maker, were we to convince ourselves that he too was a

ject. To these questions, however, Spinoza would return a single answer. To be good, to be free, to be blessed mean one and the same thing. It is a divine thought, if only it can be made to appear.

First then let us note that we habitually distinguish the forms of life as higher and lower; the grain of corn is lower than the bee, the bee is lower than the man. If we ask ourselves what we mean by this distinction, we shall find I think that we refer to the difference of the degree to which these forms are capable of carrying out a given purpose whatever the environment. The biologist would say they differ in adaptability. Take merely the common end of self-preservation: the grain of corn is lost if it fall on rocky ground or among the thorns. It can do nothing to save itself. To the bee these circumstances are indifferent, yet it in turn would succumb to a blight of the flowers. To the man, this would be but a small matter and we enjoy losing ourselves in admiration of the ingenuity with which he manages to subsist under the most unusual and threatening conditions. In a word, the higher the form of life, the greater the freedom from environment; the lower, the greater the bondage to circumstance.

What now in the future of a thing determines its degree of freedom? Spinoza studies the question only within the domain of human life. Within this domain his answer is striking: Freedom comes with knowledge; ignorance is bondage.

But there is more than one sense in which this saying may be taken. We have for example the Baconian thought, " knowledge is power." That is, given any end to be striven for, other things being equal the one who brings science to bear is the more likely to conquer circumstances, to triumph, to be free. This sense of the power of knowledge is not lacking in Spinoza.

But the freedom that comes with knowledge may be of a higher kind than the mere bettering of our chances of success. After all, human skill is extremely limited; defeat is every man's portion, and one of the most important questions in life is how to bear failure.

If knowledge is our best arm to ward off defeat, so is it our best solace when defeat, the inevitable, comes. For do we but understand that the fate that has come upon us was not to be escaped but was imposed by the eternal laws of nature, repining becomes impossible. Pain is a fact, we cannot escape it altogether, we cannot deny it when it has seized us. We *can* though prevent the sourness and bitterness that the ignorant fall prey to when they suffer. For pain is one thing, hate another. Pain is not to be escaped; hate may be. And the way to kill

difficult, since it is so rarely found. For if salvation were easily attained and could be found without great labor, how could it be neglected by nearly every one? "

Had Spinoza maintained that not only knowledge but the pursuit of knowledge was blessed, then indeed salvation must lie at every man's door. For is not life itself one long education? And if it bring its share of disillusionment, may we not repeat the words of a distinguished German scientist of our own day, "All disillusionment is enlightenment"? And this I think is the burden of Spinoza's teaching: " Let the pain of life teach you to understand and you will not hate life, but in the joy of understanding, love it."

You will learn to love life! But Spinoza has a loftier word for it: You will learn to love God. A clearing up of this expression may well end our account of the religion of Spinoza. You must recall our saying that for Spinoza and his fellow rationalists, all truths were deducible from the single one " God is," as all theorems of geometry are proved from its axioms. If the truths respecting triangles follow from the nature of a triangle and are not merely the result of physical measurement, so too, the truths about the world follow from the nature of God and are not merely brute facts that we have to accept because we are continually bumping against them. To understand a particular experience is to recognize God as its cause. But we have seen that such understanding is the greatest happiness that can come to man, for it is his assurance of power, of freedom from pain. Now Spinoza defines love as "pleasure accompanied with the idea of an external cause." If understanding is pleasure, and if it is at the same time recognition of God as a cause, it fulfils the condition of being love, and of course, love of God. It is this love of God that is at once knowledge, freedom, virtue and blessedness. "For blessedness," our philosopher has written, "blessedness is not the reward of virute, but virtue itself; nor do we rejoice in it *because* we restrain our desires, but on the contrary because we rejoice in it we are able to restrain our desires."

"I know," he writes, "that the belief of the multitude is different. Most men seem to think that they are free just in so far as they are permitted to gratify desire, and that they give up their independence just in so far as they are obliged to live according to the precept of the divine law.

"Piety, then, and religion and all things without restriction that are referred to as greatness of soul, they regard as burdens; and they hope after death

III

A DISCIPLE OF SPINOZA
An Illustration

freedom, while not denying his apparent subjection to the universal and necessary laws of physical nature. It was by this promise of freedom that Fichte was moved to the enthusiasm, the gratitude, the tears of which I have spoken.

If I have mentioned these matters, it is not because our present reflections are to dwell upon the philosophy of Fichte, nor yet upon the historic contrast between Spinoza and Kant. It is rather because the seriousness with which Fichte faced the issue between these two thinkers is shared by the men of all times and of all countries who have given themselves to the pleasures and to the burdens of reflection. The issue was not first raised by the seventeenth century, and was not laid with the eighteenth. That it remains one of the most interesting to which we of the twentieth century can turn our attention is just the point which I wish to bring out in the form of an example — an example taken, not indeed from the technical philosophy of our day, but from a writer holding a distinguished place among its novelists. Those of you who have enjoyed the more mundane writings of M. Paul Bourget, — his " Cosmopolis," his " Coeur de Femme," his " Complications Sentimentales," — are perhaps not prepared to meet in him the philosopher and moralist that shows through his less widely known, but sometimes more admired

66

work, " Le Disciple." You will allow me, then, to present so much as is indispensable of the story of Bourget's " Disciple."

Let me begin by giving some idea of the way in which the plot of the tale may have worked itself out in the author's mind. If a mass of rock were to fall from a cliff, and at its foot to crush before your eyes a human being — and not a mere vague humanity, but, let us say, a young girl just entering upon the promise of life — you would, of course, feel the full horror of the catastrophe. More than that, you would not be a descendant of the myth-makers, as we all of us are, were you not to cast about for some soul in the order of things on whom to blame the calamity as though it were a crime. Such shadowy beings from out of the past as the Fates, the " purblind doomsters," are creatures of this human instinct to transform physical nature into a moral being. But it is no longer easy to take these inventions of our fancy as seriously as did our forefathers. Galileo and Newton have come between us and the myth-makers. They have enabled us, and at the same time have constrained us, to envisage the event I have just depicted as essentially a conflict between gravitational and elastic forces, not one between the human soul and the soul of Fate. The

ern this immense universe. Tell me that I am not a monster, that there is no such thing as a monster, that you will still be there when I come out of this supreme crisis to welcome me as your disciple, as your friend."

What, then, is the philosophy of this Adrien Sixte that, having brought a human being to such a pass, it could still be appealed to to bring him through?

Adrien Sixte had made two contributions to philosophy. The first was a negative analysis of what Herbert Spencer calls the Unknowable. "Many excellent minds," the author assures us, "catch a glimpse of the probable reconciliation of science and religion on this ground of the Unknowable. For M. Sixte it is a last illusion which he is hot to destroy with an energy of argument that has not been equalled since Kant."

"M. Sixte's second title to honor as a psychologist consists in a quite new and ingenious development of the animal origin of human sensibility. . . . He undertook for the genesis of types of thought the work that Darwin essayed for the forms of life. Applying the laws of evolution to all the facts that make up the human heart, he thought to show that our most exquisite sensibilities, our most delicate moral discriminations, as well as our most shameful degradations, are the final development, the ultimate metamorphosis of very simple instincts, themselves transformations of the properties of the primitive cell: in such wise that the moral universe exactly reproduces the physical, and that the former is only the consciousness, now painful, now ecstatic, of the latter."

We owe to M. Sixte some phrases that translate with extreme energy this conviction that all is necessitated in the soul — even the illusion that the soul is free.

" Every act," he writes, "is but an addition. To say that it is free, is to say that there is in a sum more than there is in the elements added. This is as absurd in psychology as in arithmetic."

And elsewhere he put it thus: " If we knew truly the relative position of all the phenomena which constitute the actual universe, we could at this moment with a certainty equal to that of the astronomers, tell the day, the hour, the minute at which, say, England will evacuate India, when Europe will have burned its last lump of coal, when such a criminal, still to be born, will assassinate his father, when such a poem, yet to be conceived, will be composed. The future is contained in the present as all the properties of a triangle are contained in its definition."

The provenance of this type of thought is ob-

throughout the animal kingdom. "It is the law of the world," he reasons, "that all existence is a conquest carried on and maintained by the stronger at the expense of the weaker. This is as true of the moral universe as of the physical. There are souls of prey as there are wolves, tiger-cats, and hawks," and he kept repeating to himself, "I am a soul of prey, a soul of prey," with a furious access of what the mystics call *the pride of life*.

But if the animal instincts are the most widely related of those that display themselves in human conduct, more special instincts must be appealed to to account for what is special in the act. Well, in its proper place we find that the family of Robert Greslou had its roots in war-trodden Lorraine. Of no very remote peasant origin, son of a conquered race, he catches himself at certain moments reacting with instinctive hate toward an individual whom he hardly knows and who has done him no personal injury, yet whose every aspect shows him to have sprung from the conquerors, in whose most courteous gesture there lurks a polished insolence of aristocracy.

When, then, a human pity for his prospective victim comes upon this "soul of prey," it is such a hate that neutralizes it. "Why," he cries, "in so many of my imaginings does Charlotte appear by the side of her brother André? What secret fibre of hatred had this man by his mere existence touched in my heart, that simply to imagine him with his sister dried up the fountain of my pity and left nothing in me but the will to win? "

In answer we are expected to recall the moment when Robert Greslou, introduced into the family of the Marquis de Jussat as tutor to the younger son, finds himself for the first time in the presence of the Comte André, heir and dominating spirit of the house. " I felt then," our young analyst records, " in its full force, in the depths of that instinct of life into which it is so hard for thought to descend, the revelation of that sense of race which modern science attributes to all nature, and which consequently must be found in man. . . . Why should not this hostility be an heredity like the rest? The horse that has never approached a lion trembles with fear when his stall is made up with straw on which such a beast of prey has lain. Then fear is inherited, and is not fear a form of hate? Why should not hate be inherited too? And in a thousand cases envy is probably nothing but that — was nothing more than that in my case, certainly, — the echo in us of hatreds long ago acquired by those whose sons we are, and which continue in us the battle of hearts begun hundreds of years ago."

No less carefully does our author work out another group of influences: those that fall within the experience of the individual. Influences of family, of school, of books read, of friends, of adventures of sex, of religious education, all culminating in the forming of a character whose foundations have already been laid in its heredities, in this case a type for which the French have invented the expressive term, a *cérébral*. The rest one can readily imagine, the delicate suggestions of daily life, the influences, slight in themselves, that play upon the attuned character and to which it resounds with acts of this kind or that, an instrument touched by the fingers of Fate.

Such, then, is our author's understanding of what it means so to explain a human act that it shall appear to follow inevitably from recognized laws of nature. If it do so follow, we ask again: Can it in the end be regarded as either good or bad?

It is not to our author that we may turn for an answer. M. Bourget is an artist, and owes his allegiance to the interests of the heart, not to the curiosities of the intellect. For him it is sufficient to have shown that to have lived out a Spinozistic philosophy would in extreme cases lead to very ugly results. He is addressing himself, as he tells us in his preface, to the youth of France, and it may not be without interest to note the place he gives to the type of philosophy we have just been considering among the influences dangerous to the young France of his day.

"There are two types of young men," he says, "that I see before me at the present moment, which are before you too, as two forms of temptation equally redoubtable and dangerous. The one is cynical and by preference jovial. He has, since his twentieth year, discounted life, and his religion is contained in the single word, *to enjoy*, — which is translated by this other, *to succeed*. Whether he go into politics or business, literature or art, sport or industry, whether he be an officer, diplomat, or lawyer, he has only himself for god, for beginning and for end. This young man is a monster, is he not? For it is to be a monster, to have lived but twenty-five years and to have by way of a soul a calculating machine at the service of a pleasure-machine. Yet I fear him less for you than I do a certain other type. This one has all the aristocratic traits of nervous organization, all those of mentality. He is an intellectual and refined epicure, as the first was a brutal and scientific epicure. This delicate nihilist, how unpleasant he is to encounter, and how he abounds in the land! At twenty-five years he has made the tour of all ideas. His critical spirit, precociously awakened, has grasped the last results of the most subtle philosophy of this age. Do not speak to him of impiety or materialism. He knows that the word *matter* has no very precise sense. He is, on the other hand, too intelligent not to admit that all religions may have been legitimate in their time, only he has never believed and never will believe any one of them any more than he will ever believe in anything in particular, if not in the amusing play of his mind which he has transformed into an instrument of elegant perversity. Good and evil, beauty and ugliness, vice and virtue appear to him objects of simple curiosity. The human soul is for him a clever mechanism which it amuses him to take apart by way of experiment. To him nothing is true, nothing is false; nothing is moral, nothing is immoral. He is an egoist, subtle and refined, whose one occupation lies in adorning his Self, in dressing it out with new sensations. The religious life of humanity is for him only a pretext for such sensations, as is the intellectual life, as is the life of feeling. His corruption is vastly more profound than that of the barbarian of pleasure, is vastly more complicated, and the pretty name of dilettantism with which he covers it hides its cold ferocity, its appalling hardness. Ah, we know him too well, this young man; we have all just missed being such as he is, we whom the paradoxes of too eloquent masters have too much charmed. We have all *been* this man for a day, for an hour, and if I have written this book, it is to show you, you who are not yet like him, child of twenty whose soul is yet in process of making, what base things such egoism may hide in its depths."

For Bourget, then, to have justified this picture of the youthful Spinozist, is enough. But for us, who for the moment have become philosophers, who have given ourselves up to the curiosities of the mind, it is not enough to have convinced ourselves that certain teachings are ugly and unpleasant to contemplate; we must know whether they are true or false. While much that is unlovely is also untrue, who but the poet can feel sure in his heart that only the beautiful is true? Well, then, if we were to face the issue that seems to be drawn between that universal necessity which science hopes to establish throughout the domain of nature, and that freedom which ethics regards as indispensable to the existence of moral beings, — if we are to face this issue squarely, on which side should we range ourselves?

I answer: On both sides. If you say: But this is difficult to do, I should not be inclined to dispute it; were it otherwise, opinions on this subject would not be so much at variance. Yet it may not be impossible to do. And that the satisfaction of the result has been thought to be worth any effort it may cost to reach it, is evidenced by the long struggle which the history of human reflection records, to hold at the same time the vital ideals of science and the no less vital ideals of morality. To consider a way in which I believe this may be done, will occupy us throughout the remainder of the present discussion.

Let us begin by making clear just what *is* the ideal which guides the scientist in his expectations respecting the world he studies. Perhaps no one accomplishment of science has been more inspiring than the picture of certain large aspects of nature that Newton succeeded in drawing, — such aspects, namely, as are presented in the behavior of suns, and planets, and moons. All these huge masses are governed by a single law, called the law of gravitation. Now to say that they are governed by this law means no more than this, that if we knew the mass, the position, and the velocity of each of these heavenly bodies at a given moment, we should be able by means of the law to predict their masses, positions, and velocities for all future moments. This result is, to be sure, only an approximation, for we know that gravitation is not the only force which bodies exert on each other. We have never succeeded, *e.g.*, in reducing the attractions and repulsions of electrified bodies to gravita-

tion, nor do we any longer try to do this. But Newton's degree of success provides us with an ideal to
which we seem ever more and more closely to approach. Instead of considering such huge bodies as
suns and planets and their satellites, we divide these
up into extremely minute parts, which we may call for
the moment *atoms*. We struggle then to conceive a
law as completely determining the behavior of these
atoms, as the law of gravitation determines that of
planets. So that, if we knew a limited number of
characteristics of each of these atoms at a given moment, our law would enable us to predict their future
and to reconstruct their past history. As we approach more and more closely to this ideal, less and
less in the behavior of these small parts of nature
is left to guess-work. In so far as we hope this ideal
may be continuously approached, we hope that in its
atomic parts nature is entirely devoid of freedom.
And if we hope this, we must inevitably hope, too,
that what we have called an atom is neither a moral
nor an immoral being. This hope is usually called
the mechanical ideal, and nature in the light of it is
viewed as a mechanism. It has guided science to victory after victory, and I venture to think that no
result of philosophical experience is more firmly established than this, that whatever theory we may in
the end accept respecting human nature, its freedom,

its moral responsibilities, no assumption of that theory may stand in contradiction with the mechanical ideal. To have recognized this truth and to have had the courage to maintain it at all costs, was the heroic service rendered by Spinoza at a moment in human history when such service was badly needed. It is also the reason why Spinozism, in spite of its apparently gloomy outlook upon the world, has made such a forcible and lasting appeal to the imagination of thinking men. In what follows it is against certain false implications that have been thought to lie in this mechanical ideal, and not against the ideal itself, that our criticism must be directed.

Now there is one implication that lies so near the surface I doubt not most who have followed so far will already have drawn it. If, namely, the atoms of which we have spoken are bound by strict mechanical law, if it is these same atoms that make up the human body and that are concerned in its every act, must not the conduct of that body be an outcome of this same mechanical necessity? And if this be so, must not the science whose ideal we have described set itself once for all against the hope of finding in human conduct any vestige of freedom, any trace of moral responsibility? You remember with what vigor Adrien Sixte drew this very conclusion. "Every act," he said, "is but an addition.

To say that it is free, is to say there is in a sum more than there is in its elements added. This is as absurd in psychology as in arithmetic."

Yet natural as this inference may seem, we should, I think, see that it is unjustified, that the instinct which has led mankind to read moral aspects into nature was possessed of a deeper insight than was our philosopher with his plausible mathematics. If, indeed, we could construct the notion of a man out of that of atoms by a process of addition, we could not escape the conclusion of Adrien Sixte. Then, truly, moral aspects would be as completely lacking to the whole being as they are to the atoms which enter into his composition. That we cannot do this, — that we can, indeed, offer no mechanical definition of life, is just the insight which permits us, nay, practically forces us, to treat man as a free moral agent.

We can frame no mechanical definition of life! Nor is this the only example offered by experience of a term applied exclusively to mechanisms and yet meaning nothing mechanical. Let me give a homely illustration. There is, I presume every one would admit, no time-piece which is not a machine. And yet we can offer no mechanical definition of a time piece, for the simple reason that the various machines to which this term applies have no mechanical principle in common. A class which may include such divers mechanisms as a sun dial, an hour glass, a water clock, a pendulum clock, a spring watch, a chronograph, has evidently not been given a single name to mark in the members composing it a single mechanical nature. The only thing these members have in common is a certain function or purpose, — that of producing a movement keeping pace with the apparent motion of the sun. Just so with the class of beings we call living. Each of them at each moment of its existence is a complete illustration of mechanical law, yet all of them offer such divers illustrations of this law that they cannot have been put into a single class because of a common mechanical nature. That which they have in common, by virtue of which they have been grouped under one name, is once more a function or a purpose. For we observe that living things, by whatever mechanical devices, accomplish for the most part a common result, that of self-preservation.

In these two examples, the one taken from the inanimate, the other comprising the animate world, we see how well it may come about that a certain character belong to a whole, no vestige of which is to be found in its constituent parts. A single atom cannot, if the mechanical ideal is maintained, be re-

highest form of deliberate human behavior. If we consider the explanation which our author offers of the conduct of his unhappy hero, we see that in the end he has been exclusively interested in pointing out the motives to which the young man reacted. To point out motives is simply to recognize the end for the sake of which the act is accomplished. Now, although this type of explanation is in daily use among all men of all times, it was not erected into a scientific system before the reflections of Plato and Aristotle had shown of what extension it was susceptible. Aristotle in particular is responsible for having pushed to the very limit the notion that the greater part of nature's happenings can be explained in terms of the end for the sake of which they occur. The whole drama of nature was to him what that of organic life is to most of us, the struggle of individual beings to accomplish their natural purposes. But, interested as Aristotle was in pushing this concept of purpose in nature to the limit, he could not blind himself to the fact that no purpose could be found in nature which was always and invariably accomplished or attained by the beings whose nature it was to struggle for it. Consequently, he was in the habit of saying that "laws of nature (by which he meant of laws of purpose) were descriptions of what happens always, or for the most part." That is

May we not then sum up our conclusions in some such form as this? — Mechanical laws *do* completely determine the conduct of everything to which they may be applied, but they cannot be applied to an animate being, since no mechanical definition of such a being is possible. Laws of purpose *can* be applied to such a being, but they do not completely determine his conduct. It is because the only law which can thus apply to a human being does not necessitate his behavior, that we are obliged to regard that behavior as free and the being himself as responsible. The most that we can do in terms of such laws is to calculate the *chances* for or against the individual's success, for or against his ultimate worth.

Here let us stop. Our discussion shows signs of falling into the abstract and mathematical, and one may wonder whether anything practical can come of it. One will recall the unhappy disciple of Adrien Sixte, and will ask onself: What answer, after all, are we return to his cry, " De profundis! " Can we offer him any solace in his wretchedness? I think we can, only it is not the kind of solace he asks for, nor can it come from the direction in which he seeks it. I should be inclined to say to him, to Fichte in his Spinozistic mood, to any other over whom the mechanical ideal hangs heavily: This ideal is a safe guide in all thinking for which it has a meaning; no atom in your body nor out of it, but what is determined by mechanical necessity; but the sum of these atoms is not you; there is a difference between the whole we call a man, and the sum of the atoms that make up the machine that is to him. These atoms may come and go, the man remains. What constitutes his nature as a living being, an animal, a man, can receive no definition in terms of the atoms now in his body, nor those that may later take their place. You as living, as animal, as man, can be defined only in terms of the ends common to the individuals of these classes. In so far as thus natured, you fall under laws not of a mechanical order. They are laws of average which determine not you, but your chances of accomplishing the ends that define your being. In so far as you accomplish such ends, you are good of your kind; in so far as you fail, you are evil, — and if you fail egregiously enough, you are a monster. The most your self-analysis could have made out by the way of excuse is that the chances were against you. And this indeed you may have made out, for who could maintain that all men have equal chances in this world? But to have had the chances against you, is not to have been determined as a falling rock is determined; there is no chance for it.

IV

DAVID HUME
1711–1776

man without making it dependent on God. It is, then, as an expression of a common enough idea, but as an uncommonly good expression of this idea, that I have settled upon David Hume for our third illustration of modern thought.

It has for some time been rather the fashion to find the grounds of a man's scientific beliefs in his personality and in the character of the environment in which he lives. And doubtless thinking, like any other activity, has its psychology, an insight into which is helpful enough, though it is notoriously easy to find that characteristic *après coup* which we should never have been able to predict beforehand.

When I say, then, that Hume had many human traits reminding us of the Philosophers of the Garden whose science is so sympathetic with his own, it must not be supposed that only such as are of like easy habit of body and companionable temper of mind should take to his principles. But it is interesting to note, after having followed the furious career of Bruno, looked in on the sober reclusion of Spinoza, that a different type of man may utter great thoughts; the type that could look back, at fifty-eight years, on a life well filled with profitable industry, and forward to one thus comfortably pictured in a letter to a friend: " I have been settled here [in Edinburgh] for two months, and am here body and soul, without casting the least thought of regret to London, or even Paris. I live still, and must for a twelvemonth, in my old house in James's Court which is very cheerful and even elegant, but too small to display my great talent for cookery, the science to which I intend to addict the remaining years of my life! I have just now, lying on the table before me, a receipt for making *soupe à la reine,* copied with my own hand; for beef and cabbage (a charming dish) and old mutton and old claret nobody excels me. I make also sheep-head broth in a manner that Mr. Keith speaks of it for eight days after; and the Duc de Nivernois would bind himself apprentice to my lass to learn it. I have already sent a challenge to David Moncreiff: you will see that in a twelvemonth he will take to writing history, the field I have deserted; for as to the giving of dinners, he can now have no further pretensions. I should have made very bad use of my abode in Paris if I could not get the better of a mere provincial like him. All my friends encourage me in this ambition, as thinking it will redound very much to my honor."

These " friends " to whom Hume refers, were at that time, as they had been throughout his life, the best of good company, that is, the kind for whom a good dinner would have been nothing had not good

" O! how I long to see America and the East Indies revolted, totally and finally — the revenue reduced to half — public credit fully discredited by bankruptcy — the third of London in ruins, and the rascally mob subdued! I think I am not too old to despair of being witness to all these things." This, to his friend Sir Gilbert Elliot in 1768. It is curious to note that Hume lived just long enough to have heard of the signing of the *Declaration of Independence*.

If, then, something of the nonchalance with which Hume throws off comfortable tradition is due to his personal character, much may be gathered respecting his motives for so treating common opinion from a study of his philosophical ancestry. For Hume is the *fine fleur* of a growth flourishing in the England of the 17th and 18th centuries, which in contrast to the Rationalism of the Continent, is usually called Empiricism. We find anticipations of an empirical philosophy in Bacon and Hobbes; but perhaps we should regard John Locke as the real founder of the school. Rationalism, as we saw in connection with Descartes and Spinoza, was inspired by the example of the mathematicians to hope that all science might be, as their science seemed to be, deduced from axioms called self-evident. These axioms appeared to be something more than the mere summing up of experiences. Between the undependable predictions of a weather prophet, who has frequently observed that a " twinge of rheumatism means coming storm," and the confidence of the geometer that if two angles of a triangle measure 120° the other will be found to measure 60°, there seemed to the rationalist not merely a difference in degree of certainty, but a difference in kind of evidence. The former knowledge, unsatisfactory as it was, could only come after experience; the latter, beautiful in its precision, would seem to be at the command of a thoughtful man before experience. Hence, for the rationalist, experience fell to the level of a mere *suggestor* of truth, an awakener of thought; reason alone could *demonstrate* the suggestion.

In complete contrast with such a view-point, the empiricist came in the end to make experience the sole test of truth, even of such truth as the mathematician possessed. If the issue is between taking thought respecting all things with the rationalist, or everywhere trusting to observation with the empiricist, it is clear the latter has plausibility on his side. Who, closing his eyes and reasoning it out, could learn that there were just eight planets, and not seven or nine? If we must do one thing or the other exclusively, is it not easier to imagine that the

are found agreeable to the laws of nature, and there is required a violation of these laws, or in other words, a miracle to prevent them? Nothing is ever esteemed a miracle if it ever happen in the common course of nature. . . . There must, therefore, be a uniform experience against every miraculous event, otherwise the event would not merit that appellation. And as a uniform experience amounts to proof, there is here a direct and full *proof*, from the nature of the fact, against the existence of any miracle; nor can such proof be destroyed or the miracle rendered credible, but by an opposite proof which is superior.

"The plain consequence is (and it is a general maxim worthy of our attention), 'That no testimony is sufficient to establish a miracle, unless the testimony be of such kind that its falsehood would be more miraculous than the fact which it endeavors to establish.'" And Hume illustrates — "When anyone tells me that he saw a dead man restored to life, I immediately consider with myself whether it is more probable that this person should either deceive or be deceived, or that the fact which he relates should really have happend. I weigh the one miracle against the other; and according to the superiority which I discover I pronounce my decision, and always reject the greater miracle. If the falsehood of his testimony would be more miraculous than the event which he relates; then, and not till then, can he pretend to command my belief or opinion."

As a specimen of the manner in which Hume would have one weigh the probabilitites for and against miracles, we may take the oft-cited passage with which the discussions closes. ". . . Let us examine those miracles related in scripture; and not to lose ourselves in too wide a field, let us confine ourselves to such as we find in the *Pentateuch,* which we shall examine, . . . not as the word or testimony of God himself, but as the production of a mere human writer and historian. Here, then, we are first to consider a book presented to us by a barabarous and ignorant people, written in an age when they are still more barbarous, and in all probability long after the facts which it relates, corroborated by no concurring testimony, and resembling those fabulous accounts which every nation gives of its origin. Upon reading this book, we find it full of prodigies and miracles. It gives us an account of a state of the world and of human nature entirely different from the present; of our fall from that state; of the age of man extended to nearly a thousand years; of the destruction of the world by a deluge; of the arbitrary choice of one people as the favorites of heaven, and that people the countrymen of the author; of their deliverance from bondage by prodigies the most astonishing imaginable: I desire any one to lay his hand upon his heart, and after a serious consideration declare whether he thinks that the falsehood of such a book, supported by such testimony, would be more extraordinary and miraculous than all the miracles it relates; which is, however, necessary to make it to be received, according to the measure of probablity above established."

Higher critical ability and wider knowledge have since Hume's day been brought to bear upon the interpretation of such documents as the books of the Old Testament, and it is not as an ethnologist that he has any claim upon our attention. But the citation will serve to show that the skepticism of the empirical method is not of a kind greatly to disturb our confidence in the commonly accepted laws of nature. It will further serve to establish one point respecting Hume's theology, a point which throughout all his hesitating utterances on this subject he never abandons, that, namely, if aught in the world as we know it points to a God, it is not the strange and exceptional, but the regular and law-abiding aspects of nature. To him, a wonder-working God is a superstition of the ages of ignorance and of the ignorant of all ages.

" Even at this day, and in Europe," he writes in

his " Natural History of Religion," " ask any of the vulgar, why he believes in an omnipotent creator of the world; he will never mention the beauty of final causes, of which he is wholly ignorant. He will not hold out his hand, and bid you contemplate the suppleness and variety of the joints in his fingers, their bending all one way, the counterpoise which they receive from the thumb, the softness and fleshy parts of the inside of his hand, with all other circumstances which render that member fit for the use to which it is destined. To these he has been long accustomed, and he beholds them with listlessness and unconcern. He will tell you of the sudden and unexpected death of such a one; the fall and bruise of such another; the excessive drought of this season; the cold and rains of another. These he ascribes to the immediate operations of providence; and such events as with good reasoners are the chief difficulties in admittting a supreme intelligence, are with him the sole arguments for it."

But, he adds on this occasion, " many theists, even the most zealous and refined, have denied a *particular* providence, and have asserted that the Sovereign mind or first principle of all things, having fixed general laws, by which nature is governed, gives free and uninterrupted course to these laws, and disturbs not, at every turn, the settled order of events by particular volitions. From the beautiful connection, say they, and rigid observance of established rules, we draw the chief argument for theism; and from the same principles are enabled to answer the principal objections against it."

It is in this " refined " variety that we shall expect to find Hume in the end, if among theists at all. Meanwhile it will be interesting to follow up this reference to a particular providence, belief in which Hume associates so closely with the acceptance of miracles.

Section XI of Hume's " Enquiry Concerning Human Understanding," is entitled " Of a Providence and of a Future State." A literary device puts the argument in the mouth of a friend who has been invited by one referred to in the first person to imagine himself making a speech for Epicurus before an audience of enlightened Athenians. Accepting the challenge the friend opens his apology as follows: " The religious philosophers [O, ye Athenians], not satisfied with the tradition of your forefathers and doctrine of your priests (in which I willingly acquiesce) indulge a rash curiosity in trying how far they can establish religion on the principles of reason; and they thereby excite, instead of satisfying, the doubts which naturally arise from a diligent and scrutinous enquiry. They paint in the most magnificent colors the order, beauty and wise arrangement of the universe; and then ask, if such a glorious display of intelligence could proceed from the fortuitous concourse of atoms, or if chance could produce what the greatest genius can never sufficiently admire. I shall not examine the justness of this argument. I shall allow it to be as solid as my antagonists and accusers can desire. It is sufficient if I can prove, from this very reasoning, that the question is entirely speculative and that when I deny a providence and a future state, I undermine not the foundations of society, but advance principles which they themselves, upon their own topics, if they argue consistently, must allow to be solid and satisfactory.

"You then, who are my accusers, have acknowledged that their chief or sole argument for a divine existence is derived from the order of nature. . . . From the order of the work you infer that there must have been project and forethought in the workman." Now, "if the cause be known only by the effect, we never ought to ascribe to it any qualities beyond what are precisely requisite to produce the effect. . . . No one, merely from the sight of one of Zeuxis's pictures, could know that he was also a statuary or architect. . . .

"Allowing, therefore, the gods to be authors

of the existence or order of the universe, it follows
that they posses that precise degree of power, intelligence and benevolence which appears in their workmanship. . . . The supposition of farther attributes
is mere hypothesis; much more the supposition that
in distant regions of space or periods of time there
has been or will be a more magnificent display of
these attributes and a scheme of administration more
suitable to such imaginary virtues. . . . Let your
gods, therefore, O philospohers, be suited to the
present appearances of nature, and presume not to
alter these appearances by arbitrary suppositions in
order to suit them to attributes which you so fondly
ascribe to your deities."

And the pleader proceeds to show that it is as useless to practice as unsupported by reason, to supplement the order of things we know by another for
which there is no evidence.

" Are there any marks of a distributive justice in
the world? " he puts it to his hearers. " If you answer in the affirmative, I conclude that since justice
here exerts itself, it is satisfied. If you reply in the
negative, I conclude that you have then no reason to
ascribe justice in our sense of it to the gods. If you
hold a medium between affirmation and negation by
saying that the justice of the gods at present exerts
itself in part, but not in its full extent, I answer that

you have no reason to give it any particular extent, but only as far as you see it *at present* exert itself."

We had rather anticipated that we should find Hume among those " zealous and refined theists " who point to the " beautiful connection " and " single plan " of nature as to the ultimate evidence of an intelligence back of it. But now that we have gathered together his important denials, we begin to feel that Hume's " zeal " for theism must be of the most restrained order, that the " refinement " of his proof must approach attenuation.

And so in the end, it proves. Not but that there are emphatic enough avowals of conviction: " The whole frame of nature bespeaks an intelligent author;" we find it written, " and no rational enquirer can, after serious reflection, suspend his belief a moment with regard to the primary principles of genuine Theism and Religion." But this firmness of assertion is not an enduring mood. Elsewhere we find at least one " rational enquirer " suspending his belief, not for a moment, but indefinitely. The essay which opens with the passage just quoted concludes with these words: " The whole is a riddle, an enigma, an inexplicable mystery. Doubt, uncertainty, suspense of judgment appear the only result of our most accurate scrutiny concerning this subject. But such is the frailty of human reason, and such the irresistible contagion of opinion, that even this deliberate doubt could scarcely be upheld did we not enlarge our view, and opposing one species of superstition to another, set them-a-quarrelling; while we ourselves, during their fury and contention, happily make our escape into the calm, though obscure regions of philosophy."

To explain this flickering mood, one is abandoned to one's own insight into the nature of the man and into the conditions of his problem. In the first connection, we make it out that Hume's genial bearing before men cloaked, in a seemly well-bred fashion, a deep seriousness of character, just as the light tone of certain of Plato's dialogues is chosen as a fit medium for the setting forth of lofty ideas in polite company. At sixteen, before he had acquired this *pudeur* of high sounding discourse, we find him writing to his friend Michael Ramsay with the shameless solemnity of a Roman sage: "The perfectly wise man that outbraves fortune is much greater than the husbandman who slips by her, and indeed that pastoral and saturnian happiness I have in a great measure come at just now — " and more of the like! We may safely take it that the sage of sixteen had not died in the man of sixty, for all that the latter preferred to talk with his worldly friends of " *soupe à la reine* and beef and cabbage (a charming dish). " Well, then, in common with most natures possessed of a like " high seriousness," Hume would have preferred to see the world in a religious light, would instinctively have looked in it too for high purpose. And this high purpose, he seemed to see it out of the corner of his eye as one does the first star in the twilight. But when he sought it with full, clear vision — it was gone.

The reason for this phenomenon may, perhaps, lie in the nature of the problem as Hume habitually thought of it. It was, there could be no doubt of it, the order and uniformity of nature that was to reveal to us an intelligent cause. But in daily life, as in the highest philosophy, we recognize two kinds of order and uniformity in our experience. It is an established rule that a stone will fall to the earth, that all stones will fall in the same way, that a single law describes a behavior common to this stone's falling and to the planets' swinging in their orbits, a law we imagine to hold for every particle of matter in the universe in its reaction toward every other, and which we call the law of gravitation. The law of gravitation is about as high an expression of a uniformity holding throughout nature as we have as yet come upon. Such laws as those of physics and chemistry are among the best attested results of experience, and we may stare at them quite boldly without fear of putting them out of countenance; but then, too, we may examine them as intently as we will without finding in them the revelation of an intelligence that framed them. For merely as such laws they make no reference to a purpose to which the mechanism they govern is adapted.

But there is quite another type of uniformity which we are ever discovering and appealing to, if not in the whole of nature, at least in many of its parts. Hume calls it " unity of plan," and he points to the general adaptation of the organs of the body to the end of preserving the life of that body. And where we find such adaptation of various means to a single end, we ascribe life and even intelligence to the organic whole. Nature, from this point of view, is full of life and intelligence. Or, rather, should we not say it is full of *lives and intelligences?* Here indeed, is the difficulty; can we treat the whole cosmos as one great organism? Can we find one supreme end that all the obvious minor ends subserve, as they in turn are served by diverse means? Or, as another similar possibility, can we establish an analogy between the cosmos and a machine of human invention, an implement of the arts, — a watch, say, to follow Paley's argument? Here, too, we must find a purpose, for a machine is not merely a mechanism— it is a mechanism with a function.

Many excellent minds have expended themselves on this problem, whose difficulty is supreme, and I think we shall not be far wrong in asserting that it is at moments when the issue presents itself in this way to Hume's mind that " doubt," as he says, " uncertainty, suspense of judgment appear the only result of our most accurate scrutiny." There seems something beyond Hume's usual imperturbability in the words with which one of his dialogues concludes: " Believe me, Cleanthes, the most natural sentiment which a well-disposed mind will feel on this occasion, is a longing desire and expectation that Heaven would be pleased to dissipate, at least alleviate, this profound ignorance, by affording some more particular revelation to mankind, and making discoveries of the nature, attributes and operations of the divine object of our faith." [1] But perhaps this is only a phrase, for nowhere else do the lips of Hume shape the words " revelation " and " faith " but that the lines of mockery are seen to form around them.

In this state of mind respecting theology, it is inevitable that Hume should struggle in quite a

[1] Dialogues Concerning Natural Religion, XII.

pagan spirit with the problem of human wisdom. Our experience of life being what it is, how may man most successfully attain to happiness, and what relation has the line of conduct which prudence would recommend to that which has been traditionally regarded as virtuous?

But first, *has* there been any one principle of conduct that defines it as virtuous; or are there as many notions of virtue as there are communities with more or less independent traditions? It is a problem of ethics upon which every inquirer from Socrates down has spent his best thought.

There is a little dialogue of Hume's that suggests the nature of the problem and hints at a solution in a way altogether charming. " My friend, Palamedes," the narrator begins, " who is as great a rambler in his thoughts as in his person, . . . surprised me lately with an account of a nation with whom he told me he had passed a considerable part of his life, and whom he found, in the main, a people extremely civilized and intelligent.

" ' There is a country,' said he, 'in the world called Fourli, no matter for its longitude and latitude, whose inhabitants have ways of thinking in many things, particularly in morals, diametrically opposite to ours. . . .

" ' As it was my fortune to come among this people on a very advantageous footing, I was immediately introduced to the best company; and being desired by Alcheic to live with him, I readily accepted his invitation, as I found him universally esteemed for his personal merit, and indeed regarded by every one in Fourli as a perfect character.' "

And we are thereupon regaled with a display of Alcheic's virtues. We accompany him first in a serenade that he offers, not indeed to his lady-love, but to a certain youth, and we learn in this connection, that Alcheic, himself, who had been very handsome in his youth, had been courted by many lovers, but had bestowed his favors chiefly on the sage Elcouf, to whom he was supposed to owe, in great measure, the astonishing progress he had made in philosophy and wisdom. " It gave me great surprise," the traveller adds, " that Alcheic's wife (who by-the-by, happened also to be his sister) was no wise scandalized at this species of infidelity."

Later it appears that Alcheic was a murderer and a parricide; and when asked what was his motive for this action, he replies coolly that he " was not then so much at ease in his circumstances as he is at present, and that he had acted in that particular at the advice of all his friends."

But that, of all his actions, which was most highly applauded by the Fourlians, was the assassination of

Usbek. "This Usbek had been to the last moment Alcheic's intimate friend, had laid many high obligations upon him, had even saved his life on a certain occasion, and had, by his will, which was found after the murder, made him heir to a considerable part of his fortune. Alcheic, it seems, conspired with about twenty or thirty more, most of them also Usbek's friends; and falling all together on that unhappy man when he was not aware, they had torn him with a hundred wounds, and given him that reward for all his past favors and obligations. Usbek "had many great and good qualities; . . . but this action of Alcheic's sets him far above Usbek in the eyes of all judges of merit; and is one of the noblest that ever perhaps the sun shone upon."

Other splendid achievements of this gentleman are recounted, and the list might have been longer had not the narrator interrupted his friend. "Pray," said he, "Palamedes, when you were at Fourli, did you also learn the art of turning your friends into ridicule by telling them strange stories, and then laughing at them if they believed you?" "I assure you," replied the traveller, "had I been disposed to learn such a lesson there was no place in the world more proper. My friend did nothing from morning to night but sneer and banter and rally; and you could scarcely ever distinguish whether he were in jest or earnest. But you think, then, that my story is improbable, and that I have used, or rather abused, the privilege of a traveller? "

" To be sure," said I, " you were but in jest. Such barbarous and savage manners are not only incompatible with a civilized intelligent people, such as you said those were; but are scarcely compatible with human nature. They exceed all we ever read among the Mingrelians and Topinamboues."

" Have a care," cried Palamedes, " have a care! You are not aware that you are speaking blasphemy, and are abusing your favorites, the Greeks, especially the Athenians, whom I have couched all along under these bizarre names I employed. If you consider aright, there is not one stroke of the foregoing character which might not be found in the man of highest merit at Athens. . . . The amours of the Greeks, their marriages (the laws of Athens allowed a man to marry his sister by the father), and the exposing of their children cannot but strike you immediately. The death of Usbek is an exact counterpart to that of Cæsar," — and so the parallel runs on until Palamedes concludes triumphantly, " I think I have fairly made it appear that an Athenian man of merit might be . . . incestuous, a parricide, an assassin, an ungrateful perjured traitor, and something else too abominable to be named and having lived in this manner, his death might be entirely suitable; he might conclude the scene by a desparate act of self-murder, and die with the most absurd blasphemies in his mouth. And notwithstanding this he shall have statues, if not altars, erected to his memory."

I need hardly say that Hume has in the " Dialogue " from which I quote made use of a pleasant artifice to force on the reader's attention the nature and difficulty of his problem: to find, namely, a common meaning for the words " virtue " and " vice," by whomsoever used; in spite of the fact that nearly kindred civilizations will be the one confident it has found virtue, where the other is certain it has found vice. " How shall we pretend to fix a standard for judgments of this nature? " he finally puts the question. " By tracing matters," he answers himself, " a little higher. . . . The Rhine flows north, the Rhone south; yet both spring from the *same* mountain, and are also actuated in their opposite directions by the *same* principle of gravity. The different inclinations of the ground on which they run cause all the differences of their courses." And one by one with admirable skill, he takes up the virtues of our friend Alcheic, which to us are such conspicuous vices, to show that under the conditions of Greek life most had a quality in common with those perhaps directly opposite acts, which, under the conditions of our life we should commend, and that quality, which is the keynote of all Hume's ethics, is "utility."

"It appears," he puts it, "that there never was any quality recommended by anyone as a virtue or moral excellence, but on account of its being *useful* or *agreeable*, to a man *himself* or to *others*. For what other reason can ever be assigned for praise or approbation? Or where would be the sense of extolling a *good* character or action, which at the same time is allowed to be *good for nothing*? All the differences, therefore, in morals may be reduced to this one general foundation, and may be accounted for by the different views which people take of these circumstances."

Given Hume's world-view, it is evident that the only ones whom we have a right to count in estimating the agreeable or disagreeable effects of our actions are such other sentient beings as experience reveals to us: to wit, our fellow humans and perhaps the higher animals. Moreover, the only period which we have a right to consider as containing a life's measure of happiness and unhappiness is that which experience confirms to us: to wit, that bounded by birth and death.

Thus defined, the calculus of utility involved in

judging the merit of an act may be difficult, but is possible of an empirical solution. There remains only one question of human destiny to be settled, but it is an important one. What, namely, is the relation between the happiness experience gives me a right to expect, and the virtue of my conduct? For Hume's ethics are not egoistic. The utility that measures the excellence of my act is not merely, nor even primarily, its agreeableness to me; but also, and perhaps in larger measure, its agreeableness to others. How for this large element of altruism in all good actions am I, the actor, to be paid, if paid I am to be? To this question Hume gives an elaborate reply in a section of his " Enquiry Concerning the Principles of Morals " entitled " Why Utility Pleases." The answer is simple enough. There is in the human heart a sentiment we call sympathy, or, to use Hume's favorite word, " humanity." To possess this sentiment is to rejoice in another's joy, grieve with another's grief. To possess such a sentiment is to possess the reward of all altruism; for happiness bestowed upon another is bread cast upon the waters that returns to us after days as few or as many as may be required to produce in our own soul the sympathetic image of the happiness we have wrought in another's.

Such is the theory of human duty and of human destiny which Hume has worked out by the method of Empiricism, which pretends not to a knowledge of God, nor of a system of things broader than the world of our experience. We may allow his own words to contrast the resulting attitude toward life and duty with the theological: "I deny a providence, you say, and supreme governor of the world, who guides the course of events and punishes the vicious with infamy and disappointment, and rewards the virtuous with honor and success in all their undertakings. But surely I deny not the course itself of events, which lies open to every one's enquiry and examination. I acknowledge that in the present order of things virtue is attended with more peace of mind than vice and meets with a more favorable reception from the world. I am sensible that according to the past experience of mankind, friendship is the chief joy of human life, and moderation the only source of tranquillity and happiness. I never balance between the virtuous and the vicious course of life but am sensible that to a well-disposed mind every advantage is on the side of the former. And what can you say more, allowing all your suppositions and reasonings?"

V

IMMANUEL KANT
1724–1804

IMMANUEL KANT

THE religion of Immanuel Kant can be put in one phrase, " We cannot know that there is a God; but we ought to live as though there were one " — the difficulty lies in interpreting the phrase.

That we cannot know there is a God is a conclusion to which we have seen the decline of rationalism and the growth of empiricism slowly tending. But that we ought to live as though there were a God — what can such a phrase mean? What manner of life does it prescribe? Above all, what sort of an *ought* is this and how does it bind us?

There is no deeper interest for Kant than that which invites one to consider the meaning of the word " ought." I say, *the* meaning of " ought," yet it may be that the word has more than one meaning. For compare these two examples of its use, — first this: If you want to bisect a line you ought to describe certain arcs and draw a certain straight line. And then this: " You ought to speak the truth."

We notice at once a rhetorical difference in these two uses of the *ought*. In the first, a certain procedure is commanded *if* and only *if* we want to bisect a line. Leave out the condition this *if* introduces, and the *ought* with all that follows on it loses its meaning. No decalogue could be imagined to contain among its commands an injunction to describe arcs and draw lines. Let us call this use of the *ought* the hypothetical use, let us call the command such an *ought* introduces a hypothetical command or in Kant's own phrase a "*hypothetical imperative.*" An *ought* that is inseparable from an *if* is a hypothetical imperative.

On the other hand when I say, "You ought to speak the truth," "You ought not to steal," I seem to be using the *ought* in a sense that needs no *if* to make its meaning clear. More than that, attempts to supply an *if*, so far from making the meaning of the *ought* clearer, have more often than not the effect of changing, of travestying the meaning we instinctively see in it. Truthful speaking and honest dealing be indeed useful devices for getting along in the world, but one who is honest because honesty is the best policy seems to us hardly honest — at all events he seems to have missed the point that honesty is enjoined on us without *ifs* or *buts*. The obligation to be honest is an unconditional command, a "*categorical imperative.*" It is of such stuff as decalogues are made on — it is so the voice of duty speaks in us.

It needs no pointing out that so far as our examples go, the hypothetical ought has no moral flavor. No sin attaches to one who has left undone the things he ought to have done *if* he aimed at bisecting a line. Sin does attach to one who has done what he ought not to have done in the way of lying, no matter what end seemed to justify the means. This hypothetical *ought* finds its reason in pure science, this categorical in pure morality.

All this is true, and yet one would form a poor opinion of Kant's thoroughness if one represented him as having rushed from one or two examples to the generalization: All hypothetical uses of the *ought* are scientific and non-moral; all categorical uses are moral and non-scientific. To such a generalization Kant does indeed come, and to it he clings through difficulties more than enough to discourage one in whom the conviction of its truth were less a matter of heart than it was to Kant. But however it fitted in with Kant's character to view the command of duty as sternly categorical, it was equally part of his character patiently to seek a reason for the faith that was in him.

If Kant had wished to establish no more than that there must be *something* categorical about the moral *ought* distinguishing it from the many *oughts* that suggest nothing of morality, his task would not have been hard. For suppose that to every command there was really a hidden condition attached; suppose that the categorical was really a hypothetical imperative in disguise. Then the goodness of the act commanded could mean no more than its fitness to bring about a certain result. But what of the result? Is it, too, good? The question can obviously have no meaning, for only the way can be good; the goal cannot. And yet we seem to revolt against such meaning of goodness: there is a difference to us between a good way of cheating one's neighbor and a way of being good. Either then there is some way of defining a good end — an end which justifies the means — or else there must be a moral excellence that belongs to certain types of act irrespective of what they may lead to, if indeed they lead to aught in common. In either case we come upon the categorical *ought* — the end that ought to be pursued for its own sake, or else the type of act that ought to be followed for its own sake with no view to consequences. The first interpretation of the moral ought would be illustrated in a theory that pointed, as did Hume's, to the happiness of the community as an end imposed without condition, while it defined good actions to be such as were well calculated to bring about this end. The second interpretation is in the spirit of the Decalogue, or of the classic saying, Let justice be done though the heavens fall. It is not the business of the actor to consider the consequences of his just dealing; if the world is so divinely ordered that not the heavens but heaven's blessing fall on the just man, this is a truth to be independently established. Duty first, consequences after!

No theory of the moral *ought* can escape a recognition of a categorical command; but we must choose between the end and the act as that to which the *ought* applies. If we are sometimes doubtful whether Kant abides at all points by the decision he first makes in this matter, there can be no doubt that he comes to a decision at once in favor of the view that the moral ought applies to a type of act, not to an end this type of act might be calculated to bring about. We should still know our duty if we knew of no such end, we ought still to follow duty if there were no such end. It is in trying to carry through this idea, which we may call the Decalogue idea, of the categorical *ought*, that Kant meets his most serious difficulties. Yet the motives which made him accept and cling to such an interpretation are such as the simplest may grasp — yes, the simpler one is of heart, the more easily may one sympathize with them.

In the first place a scientific insight into the means

best calculated to bring about an end is obtainable only by study and thought. Even the simple device by which a line may be bisected is not at every one's disposal, while the highest science has but imperfect means to suggest for accomplishing the ends we most crave. But it seemed to Kant that duty must make a universal appeal, to the poor understanding as clearly as to the richly endowed; morality must be no privilege of the high, but a treasure of the humble. "Be good, sweet maid, and let who will be clever," is a word of homely counsel that has crept into our language to show how good a Kantian the plain man may be.

Or again— but really it is the same thought differently expressed — duty ought to make no hesitating uncertain appeal. No one should have a chance to excuse himself on the ground that he was ignorant of the law. But ignorance of scientific law is the portion of all of us. Alas, if we should have to grope after goodness as we do after wisdom! The intellectuality of pagan Greece might and did contemplate such a state of affairs with equanimity or even with favor. The spirit of Christianity expressed the deep desire of the unintellectual that at least virtue might be theirs for the willing.

Kant had a name for any law that was thus universal (that is, applying to everybody) and necessary (that is, free from uncertainty). He called such laws *a priori;* that is, not dependent for their authority upon the slow uncertain gathering of experimental evidence. To him then, the one chance of possessing a moral law *a priori* lay in the recognition that such a law must in decalogue fashion prescribe a type of act, not an end which might be uncertainly tried for now by truth-telling, now by lying — not an end in short which justified the means so dubiously that it might be taken to justify any means.

To us mortals wandering in the mazes of life and perplexed — we think honestly perplexed — by the way issues of right and wrong present themselves, the possession of an indubitable law of duty whose authority was higher than any consideration of consequences would be a godsend. Yet because such a thing is desirable, it does not follow that it is possible, and we are quite prepared to find Kant at this point setting up as the deepest problem of ethics the question, " How is a categorical imperative possible? " That is, what sort of a world would it be in which men recognized the authority of such an *ought* and were free and willing to obey it?

An image of one such world is the common possession of our race. God created this world, and the beings that dwell in it. On these beings he lays certain commands in the form of a decalogue, and their authority rests on the will of God regarded now as King. If God had purpose in laying these commands on his subjects, their duty to God's will must not wait on their insight into his purpose and their acceptance of it as theirs. Man has been created free to obey or not to obey God's commands, and is told that happiness will be meted out to him in the measure of his obedience, unhappiness in the measure of his disobedience. But to deserve reward, he must not only obey God's law, but do it uniquely because it is God's will. He must conceive himself as prepared to obey without promise of reward or threat of punishment. Moreover, it is not pretended that this justice will accomplish itself within the limits of human life on this earth, but in a future life and in another world whose existence must be taken on faith. Here then we have an image of a world in which a categorical imperative in the form of a decalogue is possible, and not only is possible, but has exactly the relations to purpose and to happiness that Kant required of such an imperative. Duty may serve a purpose; but the assurance we have of this is no part of the authority duty has for us. The performance of duty may bring happiness; but duty would remain authoritative if we knew nothing of any happiness it would bring.[1]

This world, we might call it the Old Testament World, is then exactly the kind of a world in which morality as Kant defines morality could and would exist. Moreover Kant is prepared to show that it is the only kind of a world in which true morality could exist. If we are to have such a thing as a command of duty, we must have the three things characteristic of our Old Testament world-image: the freedom of man, the immortality of the soul, the ruling power of God. If we take these, as well we may, to be the essential beliefs of religion, then it appears that for Kant morality is inseparable from religion.

I say that Kant is prepared to prove that without these three assumptions, God, freedom and immortality, no categorical imperative is possible; but I am far from asserting that a conscientious thinker will be prepared to follow Kant in every step of this proof. It is in most parts a tortured process of reasoning at once over subtle and over simple, and back of it all, one feels that Kant's deepest motives

---

[1] This image of the Old Testament World is not of course supposed to be that of the ancient Hebrews. Rather does it represent this world as reflected in the thought of a modern Christian community.

for arriving at his conclusions are the instinctive demands of his heart, which demands a marvelous intellect is made to serve as best it may.

However, the first step is obvious enough: unless there is a sense in which the being on whom a duty is laid is free to follow or not to follow its command, there is no sense in which duty is possible. This ought ye to do; but alas you cannot! This ought ye to do, and besides you can't help doing it! These expressions equally rob the ought of meaning. We can quite see that without freedom, duty is meaningless. Yet the beings on whom the commands of duty are laid are men like you and me, and in such beings we notice that what freedom they have is limited in a peculiar way. We are in the habit of attributing to each a certain nature or character that we try to regard as working itself out — if not in all — yet in many and various situations. But in this attempt to explain conduct in terms of character and its expression, we are constantly baffled by what seems to us a duality or even multiplicity of characters in the same individual. In this man we explain a certain part of his conduct as the outcome of a strong imperious animality; but another part shows his passion restrained by motives of honor, kindness, sympathy. Two natures are at war in him, and as we are likely to think of one of these as more really his than the other, we represent him as struggling to conquer himself.

Well, this warfare of a man with himself is one of the commonest things in life, and life itself shows that a higher or better self may often enough win the victory over and free itself from a baser and lower disposition. But life shows too that the struggle is long and bitter, so long that a lifetime is too short a span in which to secure a complete victory. Just in proportion as the higher self is high, does the struggle grow hard and lengthen itself out. If we conceive the self whose struggles we are watching to be the moral self as Kant describes it, all the love and lust of life seem to be arrayed against it. If it is to free itself, that is if we are to become completely moral agents, not a lifetime, nor a century, nor a million years, but the whole of eternity must be allowed us for our battling. But this means that the actor must be immortal, and so it is that for Kant the possibility of a completely moral being, free to act out his moral nature, presupposes immortality.

The existence of a moral being then involves the acceptance of him as a free immortal being. But though these are important traits of the Old Testament world image which Kant is trying to show to be the only image that makes morality possible, yet the recognition of a man's freedom and immortality is not peculiar to it, but may be found in many philosophies. Both, for example, have a place in Spinoza's system which is as far as possible from giving us an Old Testament account of reality.

When we add a third condition, the ruling power of God, we have a difference indeed, but also a difficulty in understanding the necessity of the assumption. To be sure, if we add the idea of justice to that of moral worth, if we require that worth should be rewarded with proportional happiness, then indeed we should have to go beyond experience to convince ourselves that such justice obtains, and we might very well identify the ideal of justice with the idea of a God-governed world. But Kant has insisted throughout that the idea of right and the idea of reward are independent, why then are they not separable? Why in order that there may be a thing that we ought to do, must there be an assurance that we shall be happy in the doing or because of the doing of it?

It is easy to give Kant's answer to this question — it is difficult to make sure that one has understood it. His answer is simply that while morality may be the *highest* desire of the human heart, it cannot be its *whole* desire. It *must* desire happiness as well as virtue.

Kant defines the happy man as one whose desires are satisfied. But if we think of this desire as being directed toward a *type* of object, any atempt to interpret Kant's motives for introducing a God into his system must meet the obvious difficulty that since morality is the highest type of desire and since it is admitted that all are free to be moral, then the Stoic happiness in virtue is assured quite without reference to a divine government of the world.

The only way we can hope to explain in what sense the will to do one's duty cannot be a complete definition of the object of human desire is to understand that happiness depends upon our obtaining, not a type of thing, — morality or wealth or power or science — but an individual thing. Our demand for moral satisfaction may be realized in one situation as well as another. "To tell the truth," if that be all we want, lays no conditions on the particular circumstances under which we tell the truth. We want to follow a principle, and principles are abstract enough. But is it not true that the kind of desire of which finite beings have the deepest experience is bent on just those things that cannot be generalized nor made abstract? What we want in them, and that on which our happiness depends, seems to be offered but this once in all possible life, and nothing like it could be imagined that would meet our desires just as well.

For example, when desire is for the love of a woman, it is for the love of *this* woman, not of *some* woman. Ask such love what it sees to love in this individual that could not just as well be found in another, and the lover will laugh you out. You are not speaking his language. You are looking for qualities, types, principles — what he wants with all his soul is not a kind of a woman but just *his* woman. And to her he sings,

> Who is it says the most? which can say more
> Than this rich praise, — that you alone are you?

Or do you ask as the thing on which all your happiness hangs that death keep his hands off just this child? Then what meaning would it have for you if a condoling friend were to point out that you had other children far more remarkable? It was not for his qualities you cared when you cared for him, nor yet for his value as a unit in counting your offspring.

I don't pretend to explain why this is, or what it all means;[1] but when Kant maintains that to will a principle and nothing but a principle is not what

[1] The individuating quality of love is again discussed in Chap. X, on "Love and Loyalty."

we mean by willing, these instances of objects of desire that are purely individual and can not be reduced to principle naturally present themselves as facts of experience that may help us to catch Kant's meaning.

Of all principles of willing, the moral principle is the highest; but the willing of individual human beings cannot from its very nature be completely defined by principle. The only world in which will can have an object; *i.e.*, the only world in which there can be such a thing as will, must be a world of individual things. If it is to be a moral world, it must be possible to struggle for these individual things without disobeying the law of duty.

Happiness, defined as getting the individual thing you want, must be guaranteed, or else, since you can only want something that is individual, willing is objectless. Who or what is to guarantee that the world in which we willers of concrete things may will consistently with moral principle exists? Not experience, surely; that has a way of arranging things so that the woman one wants is just the one principle denies one; the child one has set one's heart on is just the one death has set his seal on. The chapter of " life's little ironies " is a full one. Then does it not require the guarantee of a world maker or a world ruler that life's indifference or irony have not the last word? Does not the possibility of a moral will hang upon the assurance of God? So at least for Kant, God makes goodness possible.

"God, freedom and immortality," these three are traits inseparable from a world in which duty can speak and be obeyed; the Old Testament world is not only *a* moral world, it is *the only* moral world. And if, so far, Kant has clung very closely to the Old Testament, we should find him in his later writing — his " Religion within the Domain of Pure Reason " — clinging just as closely to the spirit of the New Testament. Those who find his reasoning obscure and faulty, would explain all this in terms of his personal psychology and his early environment, for Kant was a child of that deep Pietism, one might say Quakerism, that characterizes the Germany of the eighteenth century.

But if we look upon him as the child of his age in his devotion to Christianity, he was no less profoundly influenced by that other and equally characteristic movement of his day and generation — the inheritance of Rationalism. The Old Testament and even the New Testament world images may have deep truth hidden in their symbolism — so the child of pietism would be likely to think — but

the authority of this truth was not to be sought
in revelation. It must be established, if at all, by
one's reason — so the disciple of rationalism was
bound to maintain. Now Kant is not only a rationalist, rejecting revelation as a source of authority.
He is also a critic, to whom the arguments of rationalism for the existence of God appear flimsy and
irrational. Neither in reason nor in experience can
we find grounds for accepting the existence of God
as a scientific fact. Hume could be no more convinced than Kant that no aspect of the world with
which our experience acquaints us justifies a belief
in divine purpose. Kant went further — no extension of experience in future ages could give us the
assurance we now lack. God is unknown to our
science and unknowable.

Well then, if neither the necessities of thought
nor the facts of experience, however we conceive
our knowledge of them extended, can force upon
us a belief in God and all that hangs on him, what
is left of religion and of morality that cannot be
separated from religion? Kant's answer to this
question is so confusing that it is little wonder the
interpreters of Kant are confused, in disagreement
with each other and each doubtful of himself. I
am obliged then, since we have not the time to try
out all the ifs and buts of the case, to present dog-

matically one line of thought that is to be found in
Kant, the one along which post-Kantian thought
developed. If anyone tell me that he fails to find
this thought in his edition of Kant, or that he finds
others that do not run parallel with it, we shall not
quarrel about a matter commentators have always
quarreled about.

If Kant as a critic has been keen to point out the
inadequacy of any proof of God, he has been no
less earnest in his purpose of showing that no dis-
proof can come to us. This world is one that for
aught we know *may* be God's world, and if we
choose to live as though it were God's world and
we were of his kingdom, we need fear to meet no
facts that would block our way and deny us.

Doesn't it lie near to hand to say — You can
make this God's world if you want to? You can
make yourself free, immortal and blest of heaven
if that is the deepest desire in you, for in all its
moral aspects this world of yours is a plastic world
and will respond delicately to your touch. Live
then as though there were a God, and there will
indeed be one; the world will be divine.

I have called Kant's world the Old Testament
world and you have seen in what sense it may be
called so; but if you try to think of this world as
the mediaeval writers are supposed to have thought

of it, then Kant's religion must be in flat contradiction with itself. If God is such a God, if
his creative act is such a gesture as a Michael Angelo
might paint, if life after death is such a life and
spent in such places as a Dante might describe, then
all Kant's religion is but a leap in the dark. The
thing reduces to something like Pascal's wager —
bet on God, and if you lose you lose nothing; if
you win you win everything. If God, freedom,
and immortality are facts hid behind a curtain that
we may never tear aside, we can only take a chance
with such facts. I have already made my bow to
those who find other things in Kant than the
religion I pretend to have drawn from him — and
I had particularly in mind such as understand Kant
throughout to be thinking of the truths of religion
as just such facts hid behind the curtain. I have
refused to quarrel with those interpreters because
Kant does think, because Kant can not cure himself
of thinking in such terms through many pages.
But this I take to be obvious — if this fashion of
thinking were the only one possible in view of the
situation in which science and religion find themselves, if it is not merely a peculiarity of the man
Kant and his personal psychology, then those who
followed on him, Fichte, Schelling, Hegel, were
deeply deceived in supposing that Kant was their

inspiration; the post-Kantian development was not a development but a new creation.

Viewing Kant then in the light of the appeal which he made to his own times, we may see that for him religion is not a matter of what one decides to believe, but of what one decides to do. And the religious consciousness may express the law of its doing in the determination to live as though there were a God. But we must ask it of Kant to explain to us what sort of a life this religious life would be.

One can quite make it out that the first condition to the living of such a life is to obey the voice of duty as though it were the voice of God. That is, to obey it without letting our obedience hang on our insight into the purpose to be worked out, or on the satisfaction we are to find in or because of the doing. Just so was the Decalogue presented for the acceptance of the Children of Israel. But for them the way of duty was revealed by God himself; for Kant it must be revealed by the reason which accepts it. What sort of a law does this " practical reason," as Kant calls it, reveal?

Kant's first formulation is imperfect enough, and seems to be based on an effort to deduce the content of moral law from the meaning of law itself

— as though to say, the command "Be law-abiding" furnished one with all needed information respecting the law by which one was to abide. For, as Kant puts the matter, law must prescribe a type of action that is possible for everybody — a meaning of law which is well rendered by the common phrase, "What is right for one is right for all." And just as one might try to convince a man of the iniquity of some particular act of his by putting to him the question, Suppose everybody were to do that? so Kant at this stage feels that we could try out the validity of any given type of act by putting the same question to ourselves. Suppose the right to lie were up for consideration; if lying is morally right, then it must be possible for everybody to lie. But if everybody tried to lie, there would be no such thing as a lie, for a lie requires someone to believe it as well as someone to utter it. Universal lying would be impossible; the maxim, "Be a good liar," could not be generalized into a law.

"So act that the maxim of your conduct could become a universal law." [1] This is the formula that Kant finds first of all for the full duty of man. But of course on this basis one could not sell a share

---

[1] The exact wording: "Handle so, dass die Maxime deines Willens jederzeit zugleich als Princip einer allgemeinen Gesetzgebung gelten könne." K. d. p. V., I, I, I.

of stock, for if everybody were to try it, there would be no market. On the other hand Kant himself has only a tortured and inadequate account to give of the reason why one should not commit suicide, for it looks as though we might all do that much together.

More interesting is Kant's second attempt to formulate the law of duty. Almost against his will, one would say, Kant is forced to consider the act from the point of view of its purpose. The purpose of a moral act must be such that everybody may pursue the same purpose.[2] An immoral world is one in which many want a thing that can not be shared — Kant recalls with humor the remark of King Francis, that he and his brother Charles were in perfect accord for both wanted the same thing — namely the possession of Milan. A moral world is one in which no desires are contradictory.

The moment Kant has said this he has made the

[2] Cf: " In der ganzen Schöpfung kann alles was man will, und vorüber man etwas vermag, auch *bloss als Mittel* gebraucht werden; nur der Mensch . . . *ist Zweck an sich selbst.* . . . Eben um dieser willen ist jeder Wille . . . auf die Bedingung der Einstimmung mit der *Autonomie* des vernünftigen Wesens eingeschränkt, es nämlich keiner Absicht zu unterwerfen, die nicht nach einem Gesetze, welches aus dem Willen des leidenden Subjects selbst entspringen könnte, möglich ist. . . ." K. d. p. V., 1, 1, 3.

moral world an ideal, an image of a world not identical with this present one, but into which our faith demands that the present one may by our effort evolve. It is impossible so far as I can see to make Kant's first impression of duty square with this account of it. It cannot be that duty is a simple certain command that the humblest understanding can grasp. It must be that duty is a more or less vague striving toward this ideal, a striving to make the world in which we live with one another approximate more and more closely to this beautiful republic whose motto might be modeled after Rabelais, " ' Fays ce que vouldras,' et ne nuis pas à ton voisin." [1] Religion then is the determination to allow nothing to divert us from this struggle which it would not be out of place to call the struggle after divinity. Immortality would be a direction, not a condition. Happiness — the religious happiness — the sense of the progress to which we are contributing. All this seems to flow naturally from the Kantian conception, but Kant has that in him which will not let such results follow. He stands divided against himself. His theory of duty as decalogue law, his less confident but no less enduring conception of the object of religion as facts behind a veil, stand in contradiction with his view

[1] Pierre Louÿs.

ARTHUR SCHOPENHAUER

WE live in a room that has a dark corner. The shadows are there and we know they are there; but we will not look their way. We busy ourselves with a thousand things that are doubtless important; we sit by the lamp and are doubtless full of cheerful thoughts. It is held to be wise to behave in this way, and if the things we busy ourselves with are really important then it may be admitted that our conduct is really wise. But back there among the shadows, the darkest of them all, lurks the spirit of questioning. "What is the use?" it keeps asking, "What is the use?" If we listen we are lost, yet those who have listened and lost themselves tell us that there is such peace to be had of knowing the worst that compared with it the prizes of struggling life are but children's toys.

"To see where the worst problems of life lie," writes a philosopher of our own day, "is a very black experience. And yet, so much does human reason live on insight that I have never met a man who was alive to those deepest problems and who repented him of his insight."[1]

[1] Royce.

recognizes in Schopenhauer the spirit of the fighter rather than that of the critic. He is a man of one idea, embraced as soon as encountered, then defended with boldness and eloquence and wit. Such a character hardly develops the great thinker; but it may well be possessed of a great thought. The thought of Schopenhauer is none the less great for being gloomy and repellant.

The double title, "The World as Will and Idea," hints at a double aspect that experience presents, the one to the eye of the observer, the other to the mind of the thinker. To the observing eye, it is a spread of bodies in space and time, obeying the laws of mechanical necessity; just such a world as Kant has described in his "Kritik der reinen Vernunft." Schopenhauer, following Kant, calls this the world of appearance, the phenomenal world.

But when we say "a world of appearances" we seem to hint at a something that appears, and appears not to the eye that follows the mechanical behavior of bodies in space and time but as revealed to the thought of one who asks: Wherefore this agitated phenomenon? Just as, watching my neighbor move and gesticulate, I ask myself: What is it all about? so, seeing Nature a-quiver, I ask myself: What does she mean? And just as my neighbor's conduct is understood when I have caught the purpose, the motive that inspires it, so I may be expected to have reached the " real nature " of the fleeting world if I can but find the *will* which it expresses.

It is then the World as Will that profoundly interests Schopenhauer, as it has profoundly interested all men, from the most primitive that have implored the gods, to the most cautiously reflective who, like Kant, have felt confident of at least this much, that no definition of a good life was possible that did not postulate a world-purpose.

Now the plainest man can assure himself that there are enough — alas, too many — purposes to be found in nature for the looking. There are mine and yours, that of our country, of our human race, of other races too, for the lower animals have disputed the world with us, as the vegetables have disputed it with them. But when one asks oneself: What ultimate purpose is served by all this disputing for a foothold? then indeed one's imagination is put to the test. There are too many purposes, there is too little purpose, to let this search for nature's will with us end in a quick and happy finding.

All this is matter of common knowledge and common experience, yet how few have had the

he notes with an amused cynicism, " there then remained nothing but ennui to furnish heaven with."

The survivor of the struggle for existence is on
these terms hardly a being to be envied, and the
" *terque quaterque beati* " must often come to his
lips as he recalls those who have fallen. Indeed,
it is exactly that place in the scale of existence
which gives advantage in the struggle, that brings
with it a consciousness of the vanity of this same
struggle. It is exactly to man, who in his moment
of pride has thought nature a " manufactory of
things for his use," that is given the most poignant
sense of alternating hunger and satiety. This most
necessitous of all beings " stands upon the earth,
left to himself, uncertain about everything except
his own lack and misery. Consequently the care
for the maintenance of that existence under exact-
ing demands which are renewed every day occupies
as a rule the whole of human life. To this is
directly related a second claim, the propagation of
the species. Here he is threatened from all sides
by the most different kinds of danger, from which
it requires constant watchfulness to escape. With
cautious steps and casting anxious glances around he
pursues his path — thus he went as a savage, thus
he goes in civilized life; and there is no security for
him.

ARTHUR SCHOPENHAUER

Qualibus in tenebris vitae, quantisque periclis
Degitur hoc oevi, quodcumquest.

" Life is a sea full of rocks and whirlpools which
man avoids with the greatest care and solicitude,
although he knows that even if he succeeds in getting through with all his efforts and skill, he comes
thus but the nearer at every tack to the greatest, the
total, the inevitable shipwreck, death."

And Schopenhauer rounds off the whole with
these lines, " Thus, between desiring and attaining
all human life flows on. The wish is in its nature
pain, the attainment . . . satiety: the end is an
illusion and possession takes away charm. The wish,
the need, presents itself under a new form, or when
it does not, follows desolateness, emptiness, ennui
against which the conflict is just as painful as against
want." And just as the superior animal is the most
suffering of all animals, so the superior man is the
most suffering of all men. The calm joy of science, the pleasure of the beautiful, the delight in art
— " these things demanding rare talents are granted
to very few, and to those few only as a passing dream.
And then even these few on account of their higher
intellectual power are made susceptible of far
greater suffering than duller minds can ever feel.
Moreover such men are placed in lonely isolation by

for his message. Not merely among the technical philosophers is his influence to be traced, but in that sensitive expression of what is passing in the heart of his age — the artist. Never has art had the courage it now displays to conceive the tragedy of life as Schopenhauer thought it out — not indeed the drama of guilt and its punishment, the ideal of justice working itself out at the cost of individual pain. This is the older conception of tragedy — Schopenhauer would say it is not tragedy at all. To the modern conception tragedy lies in the perception that there *is* no justice in the world — only indifference, only chance, only stupidity. One might cite works of Flaubert, tales of Maupassant, pages of Anatole France; but most notable of all, pretty much the whole literary output of Thomas Hardy, that tireless recorder of " Life's Little Ironies," that bold acknowledger of crass casualty as the only god of things. Schopenhauer does not stand alone against a background of forgotten gloom if one may still hear the voice of nature questioning as Hardy heard it:

" When I look forth at dawning, pool,
　　Field, flock, and lonely tree
　　All seem to look at me
Like chastened children sitting silent in a school.

" Their faces dulled, constrained and worn,
　　As though the master's ways
　　Through the long teaching days
　Their first terrestrial zest had chilled and overborne.

" And on them stirs, in lippings mere
　　(As if once in clear call,
　　But now scarce breathed at all)
' We wonder, ever wonder, why we find us here.

" ' Has some vast Imbecility
　　Mighty to build and blend
　　But impotent to tend
　Framed us in jest, and left us now to hazardy? '

" Thus things around.　No answer I . . . "

It is time we come to the question: What then?
Life is a misery, and then what?

" The door is open," said Marcus Aurelius. " The
door is open, if the house is smoky, leave it." It
is the solution of antiquity, and Schopenhauer himself finds it much more reasonable than most of
the reasons that have been urged against it.　Yet it
is not through this easily opened door that he sees
a way of escape from the ironic will to live.　If that
will had a date and a local habitation, then indeed
to kill the body in which it dwelt would put an end
to the monster.　But such is not the case.　Among

the accidents of time and space you happen to be one; but had you not been one, or were you no longer one, the game would play itself out by the same rules, only another pawn would be on the spot that was yours. Now the evil of the game is not that *you* happen to be one of the pieces, but rather that it should be played at all. Not the pawn, but the player must be killed, and the player is always that brutal Will to Live, pitted against itself, winning as it loses and losing as it wins. Step out of it if you will, what does he care? But stay in it, and by doing your part not with but against him you may not only emancipate yourself but have your share in putting an end to the game itself. What is this part to be played by each against the Will to Live? We shall come to Schopenhauer's account of it in due time, meanwhile it is certainly *not* the impatient gesture of self-destruction.

From the past again comes another answer to the question: What then? It takes the form of a wine song, and we catch its refrain from the lips of singer after singer. "Another and another cup," cries Omar, "to drown the memory of this insolence."

Well, for this solution too Schopenhauer has his sympathy. Not for the wine that is red, to be sure, — its intoxication is too brief, the awakening too bitter — but for the wine of beauty wherever it is to be found in nature or in art. It is most natural that Schopenhauer — for whom the woe of life springs from the possession of an aggressive, fighting selfhood — should have looked for solace to that beauty in which, we say, we forget ourselves, before which we stand rapt. The effect every one knows — the cause? That was Schopenhauer's peculiar contribution to the theory of the beautiful. In a word his explanation is this. We forget our own individuality with all its torment, because we are seduced by the beauty of the thing we look at to forget *its* individuality.

There is in the Louvre a somewhat dirty piece of marble whose size and weight with the story of how it came to be where it is, may be found in the guide books. This at least is its individual description. But to the many human beings who have stood rapt before the Venus de Milo there has appeared not this dirt, nor yet this marble, nor yet the effigy of a woman; but just the vision of womanhood. And therewith, Schopenhauer would suggest, we have taken a step out of the contentious world. It is no longer a human being but human nature we are in presence of, and to lose oneself in nature is, while the vision lasts, to have forgotten the will to live in its troublesome individuality.

While the vision lasts! But the trouble here

is that such visions will *not* last. In the contemplation of beauty we have the foretaste of peace; but not the peace eternal. And the question comes back upon us: What is to be done?

The answer now in progressive completeness comes from three sources. The first suggestion, imperfect though it is, we catch from the institution of civil law. Now law, and the penalties it provides, is a conscious effort to restrain the individual from doing wrong. " Wrong," meanwhile, Schopenhauer defines as " that quality of the conduct of an individual in which he extends the assertion of the will appearing in his own body so far that it becomes the denial of the will appearing in the bodies of others." It is then the province of law to fix as best it can the boundaries that enclose a man's rights to the exercise of his individual will and to prevent his trespassing or being trespassed upon.

But this rough and partial method of restraining the will to live from multiplying the misery which it creates in proportion as it is untrammeled is but palliative. A deeper suggestion than that offered by formal law comes from an examination of the moral sense. For the distinction between right and wrong as drawn by temporal justice is by no means identical with that between good and bad as intuited by the conscience of man. For wrong, as we have seen, means merely aggression, and right, the exercise of will that commits none of the aggressions law recognizes. But it is by no means enough to keep within one's rights to possess moral worth. "For example," our philosopher points out, "the refusal of help to another in great need, the quiet contemplation of the death of another from starvation while we ourselves have more than enough, is certainly cruel and fiendish, but it is not a wrong."

What then constitutes goodness? The quality of goodness consists in an infinite sympathy, such an intuition of the misery of others as gives us a horror of inflicting pain, a delicate skill in alleviating it. Now all the misery of life comes from the assertion of the individual will, which if justice may indeed feebly hold in check, goodness alone can effectively still by destroying the distinction between soul and soul. "To the noble man," we find Schopenhauer writing, "this distinction is not significant. . . . The suffering which he sees in others touches him quite as his own. He therefore tries to strike a balance between them, denies himself pleasures, practices renunciation, in order to mitigate the sufferings of others. He sees that the distinction between himself and others, which to the wicked man is so great a gulf, only belongs to a fleeting and illusive phenomenon. He recognizes directly and without reasoning that the in-itself of his own manifestation is also that of others, the will to live which constitutes the inner nature of everything and lives in all; indeed, that this applies also to the brutes and the whole of nature, and therefore he will not cause suffering even to a brute." And yet this conception of the good life, this living in sympathy and doing works of love, beautiful as the ideal of it is, is not the final cure for the world's misery. The will to live, even so chastened, has not lost all of its genius for harm.

" If the veil of Maya," our thinker has it, " is lifted from the eyes of a man to such an extent that he no longer makes the egotistical distinction between his person and that of another, . . . then it clearly follows that such a man, who recognizes all beings as his own inmost and true self, must also regard the infinite suffering of all suffering beings as his own, and take on himself the pain of the whole world. . . . All the miseries of others which he sees and is so seldom able to alleviate, all the miseries he knows directly, and even those which he only knows as possible, work upon his mind as his own. . . . Why should he now, with such knowledge of the world assert this very life through constant acts of will, and thereby bind himself ever more closely to it, hug it ever more closely to himself?" Should not rather, we ask, this bitter world-knowledge become a permanent and final *quieter* of all and of every volition? Should not the will now turn away from life, shuddering at the pleasures it once craved, but in which it has come to recognize that assertion of life which is the fountain of misery?

And Schopenhauer expounds his meaning in a parable. "If we compare life to a course which we must unceasingly run — a path of glowing coals, with a few cool places here and there; then he who is entangled in illusion is consoled by the cool places, on which he now stands or which he sees near him, and sets out to run the course. But he who sees through the [illusion that separates the 'here' and 'there'] and thus recognizes the whole, is no longer susceptible of such consolation; he sees himself at all places at once — and withdraws."

This is the transition from virtue to asceticism and here we have the last word of Schopenhauer's doctrine of the cure. Suicide is a mistake; enjoyment of beauty a true solace, but a momentary one. Restrictions devised by society are a corrective, but the misery they can prevent is as a drop to an ocean; morality which is at bottom a charity born of sympathy is the best the world has dreamed, it destroys more and more the individual will and makes all things one, but though men in the ideal state morality might produce would suffer together, they would still suffer, for from Schopenhauer's point of view the disjunction is final; " Either desire unsatisfied, which is pain, or satisfied desire, which is ennui."

Well, this infinite wretchedness of the man who has made the round of experience in seeking relief, who has rejected suicide, who has awakened from the dream of beauty to find the old pain still there, who has tried, then lost faith in, the devices of law, who has become at last a " Beautiful Soul," to find himself then the sharer of all the world's misery, — the infinite wretchedness of such a man is a disease, not of the wrong kind of will, but of will itself. All will is evil will, and if one would have an end of pain one must refuse to will at all; is not this, the asceticism of Indian sage and Christian saint, the oldest and the ultimate wisdom?

Schopenhauer takes his word " asceticism " quite seriously. To this last expression of human insight it no longer suffices that a man should love others as himself and do as much for them as for himself; " but there arises within him a horror of the nature of which his own (phenomenal) existence is an expression, the will to live, the kernel and inner being of that world which is recognized as full of misery. He therefore disowns his own nature which appears in him and is already expressed through his body. His body, healthy and strong, expresses the sexual impulse; but he denies the will and gives the lie to the body. It thereby denies the assertion of the will which extends beyond the individual life, and gives the assurance that with the life of this body, the will, whose manifestation it is, ceases.

"Asceticism shows itself further in voluntary poverty, which not only arises *per accidens* because the possessions are given away to mitigate the sufferings of others, but is here an end in itself, is meant to serve as a constant mortification of will, so that the satisfaction of the wishes, the sweet of life shall not again arouse the will against which self-knowledge has conceived a horror. He who has attained to this point compels himself to refrain from doing all that he would like to do, and to do all that he would not like to do, even if this has no further end than that of serving as a mortification of will."[1]

And Schopenhauer becomes the exponent of that aspect of Christianity, as of other ascetic creeds, which is so unintelligible to the pagan ideals of manhood, — the doctrine of meekness. Since the ascetic "himself denies the will which appears in his own

---

[1] Abridged.

person, he will not resist if another does the same, i.e. inflicts wrongs upon him. Therefore, every suffering coming to him from without, through chance or the wickedness of others, is welcome, every injury, ignominy, and insult; he receives them gladly as the opportunity of learning with certainty that he no longer asserts the will, but gladly sides with every enemy of the manifestation of will which is his own person."

In his manner of life the Schopenhauerian ascetic is in every detail a copy of the Eastern and Western monk. His body he nourishes sparingly, lest its excessive vigor should animate the will. When at last death comes, it is most welcome, and is gladly received as a longed-for deliverance. "For him who thus ends, the world has ended also."

"For him who thus ends, the world has ended also." The seriousness with which this statement is taken marks the difference between the two great philosophies of asceticism, the Buddhistic and the Christian. Whatever the Master may himself have taught, the Christianity of the Church, say of Augustine, is a pessimism respecting the world we know, backed by an optimism respecting the world we know not, in which however the meaning of the whole plot is made clear. The *nothingness of the world* as it appears to the eyes of the Christian ascetic is then the nothingness of *this* world, but for him who leaves it there awaits a much richer life in another. For the Buddhist saint, no optimism of this kind supplements his pessimism, no other world is called upon to explain this one, and when he leaves this one through the door of asceticism it is into the eternal peace of Nirvana, of nothingness, that he sinks.

It is the latter understanding of the outcome that Schopenhauer accepts at the hands of the mystic East. "We have recognized," he writes, "the inmost nature of the world to be will, and all its phenomena to be but embodiments of the will, and we have followed this embodiment from the unconscious working of the obscure forms of nature up to the completely conscious action of man. Therefore we shall by no means evade the consequence that with the free denial, the surrender of the will, all these phenomena are also abolished; that constant strain and effort without end and without rest at all the grades of objectivity in which and through which the world consists; the multifarious forms succeeding each other in gradation; the whole manifestation of the will and finally the universal forms of this manifestation, time and space, and also its last fundamental form, subject and object, all are abolished. No will: no idea, no world."

"Before us there is certainly only nothingness," Schopenhauer concludes, but if this prospect be anything but grateful to a man, it must be because he has not really seen or accepted the truth that Schopenhauer would demonstrate and impart. "That we abhor annihilation," he insists, "is simply another expression of the fact that we so strenuously will life." Of that folly and the pain of it enough has been said. "But if we turn our glances from our own needy and embarrassed condition to those who have overcome the world . . . then instead of the useless striving and effort, . . . instead of the never satisfied and never dying hope which constitutes the life of the man who wills, we shall see that peace which passeth understanding, that perfect calm of the spirit, that deep rest, that inviolable confidence and serenity, the mere reflection of which in the countenance as Raphael or Correggio has represented it is an entire and certain gospel; only knowledge remains, the will has vanished."

And it is exactly in this way "by contemplation of the life and conduct of saints, whom it is certainly rarely granted us to meet with in our own experience, but who are brought before our eyes by their written history, and, with the stamp of entire truth, by art, that we may banish the dark impression of that nothingness which we discern behind all virtue and holiness as their final goal, and which we fear as children fear the dark . . . What remains after the abolition of the will is for all those who are still full of will certainly nothing; but conversely to those in whom the will has denied itself, this world which is so real, with all its suns and milky-ways — is nothing."

VII
FRIEDRICH NIETZSCHE
1844–1900

FRIEDRICH NIETZSCHE

" God is dead. God is dead: He died of pity "
— the phrase runs refrain-like through the " Say-
ings of Zarathustra." It is the bright news that
Nietzsche brings as his peculiar contribution to the
cause of human hope. These are the glad tidings
for whose bringing he expects that his feet shall be
called beautiful upon the mountain. Therefore they
dance, these feet, and bear toward us one who laughs
and sings. At least Nietzsche would have us believe
that truth — his truth — " comes on light feet "
and that it steps to music. " Let the day be counted
lost," he cries, " in which we have not somewhat
danced, and let us know that truth to be false which
brings no laughter with it." Yet, whether it was
that truth — Nietzsche's truth — had somehow not
the quality of joyousness in it, or whether the poor
messenger of these " glad tidings " was the victim
of ironical chance, certain it is that his dance brought
him to the doors of the mad-house, and that behind
these melancholy doors he died.

There is however nothing but a certain strange-
ness of phrase that would lead one to associate this

particular message of Nietzsche with his later insanity. It is no new idea that God is dead, no new expectation that the news will be grateful to all who understand its import. Xenophanes near the beginning, Epicurus and Lucretius toward the end of pagan thought had brought the same intelligence. Only, according to Xenophanes the Gods had died not of pity but of vice. " Liars, adulterers, cheats are the vaunted Lords of Olympus." And according to Lucretius it was again not of pity but of their cruelty the Gods were dead, the gods of that religion

> Quae caput a caeli regionibus ostendebat
> horribili super aspectu mortalibus instans.

Nor are the ancients the only ones to whom the world has appeared godless. If for Hume God was only suspiciously silent, for Schopenhauer he was conspicuously absent. Still, it was far enough from Schopenhauer's thought that a God could die of pity. Pity was for him the one divine thing left to a God-forsaken world; it at least might soften, even if it could not cure the fundamental cruelty of life. It was rather the unreason of the world that forbade us to see in its course a divine guidance. For Schopenhauer, God had died quite mad.

Vice, cruelty, reticence, irrationality — these had

been variously recognized as ills of which a God might die. It remained for Nietzsche to suggest that the most fatal of all disorders, whether in God or man, was just that gentlest of all Christian virtues — Pity or, as the German tongue has it, Mitleid: fellow-suffering. In the understanding of the motives that led Nietzsche to this utterance lies the key to his whole philosophy — if the " lightning flashes " of his thought may, somewhat against his will, be called a " philosophy."

Virtues like races — perhaps I should say *with* races — have their ascendancy and their decline. The quality of pity is not greatly admired of strong young peoples. The virtues of triumphant pagandom were made of sterner stuff: one hears much of temperance, of courage, of wisdom, of justice; little indeed of compassion. It is with Christianity that faith, hope, and charity are introduced into our culture, and throughout Christendom the greatest of these remains charity. Thus it is that Nietzsche always refers to these virtues as the " modern idea," and since modernity is to his mind desperately sick, he seeks the cause of its disease in its " fixed idea."

Now in imagining that charity or pity might well be a symptom of weakness, Nietzsche does not stand alone even among modern thinkers. Spinoza for one is inclined to be critical of the excellence of pity. Why pity one's neighbor more than oneself? And Why pity oneself at all? Is not such self-pity a form of repining? But the cure for repining is understanding — the understanding that all things are of God. One might as well regret that the area of one's field is not greater than the product of its base and side, as that the length of one's days does not exceed three-score years and ten. And Kant again is no sympathetic witness to the virtue of pity. "There is but one thing good," he has said, "and that is a good will " — the will, namely, to obey the command of duty. If one have this one cannot need pity; if one have it not one cannot deserve pity.

But Spinoza and Kant are in this, as in other respects, exceptions to the soft mood of modern sentiment. With Schopenhauer, the very embodiment of modernity, we have seen pity once more set on high as the unselfish virtue. It is the self-less man that becomes the holy man; it is the holy man that becomes the sage, denying the world with its pitiless Will-to-live.

Now it is against this very philosophy of Schopenhauer, against this conception of the beauty and wisdom of self-surrender that Nietzsche reacts. If to Spinoza pity is a folly, if to Kant it is a superfluity, to Nietzsche it is a vice — more than a vice, a disease, that deep sickness of modernity which spells decadence. Schopenhauer, and all that older wisdom which Schopenhauer loved, of Jesus and of Buddha, these were Nietzsche's great denials, these were the false physicians of the soul that had made the soul sick in making it sad.

If Nietzsche reacts so violently against the teaching of Schopenhauer, it is not because he is by nature precluded from appreciating its seduction. It is rather because he had at one time in his life too deeply understood and too completely yielded to its soothing counsel of surrender that he later bends all his energies to its destruction. This complete revulsion of feeling was not a unique episode in Nietzsche's experience. On the contrary his intellectual life is largely a history of such accepting and rejecting. Born into a clergyman's family, passing his childhood in quiet Naumburg, Nietzsche in his last years claims the name of Antichrist. Eagerly connecting himself in his student days at Bonn with one of those corps that treasured the republican ideals of '48, he advocates in his later years a social organization modeled on the caste-system of the East. An ardent patriot in '70, he becomes the contemner of the organized state in general, a contemptuous critic of Germanism in particular. A trained student of history, a distinguished professor of philology at Basel, some of his most cunning and cutting analyses expose the weakness of the learned temperament. In his first important work, " The Birth of Tragedy," we find him an apostle of Wagner; his later " Case of Wagner " is perhaps the cruelest polemic against a man and his art of which modern letters give example.

The bare enumeration of these changes is bound to leave an impression of waywardness. Yet this impression would be in so far false that it is clear each accepting was a matter of deep feeling with Nietzsche, each rejecting cost its price. At times, to be sure, he would put on a brave front before the spectacle of his thought's inconstancy. Only those that can change can grow: " I love those that change," he writes. But at other times there is more of melancholy in his recalling of abandoned ideals. " If thinking be thy destiny, then honor that destiny with divine honors; sacrifice to it thy best and thy dearest." It is not without reason that he calls the progress of his thoughts a " Selbstüberwindung " and one may best understand the fierce bitterness of his attack upon those he has put behind him if one remember that nothing less than hatred could replace an old love in this too tenacious heart.

It is then of a piece with the rest, if a philosophy which in the end represented the dearest foe of his thought should have been the friend and guide of Nietzsche's youth. How deep a meaning Schopenhauer had once possessed for him may be judged from the following extracts. The first is from a letter written in 1867 to his friend the Baron von Gersdorff on the occasion of the death of von Gersdorff's brother:

"Perhaps this death is the greatest grief that could have come to you. And now, dear friend, you have experienced for yourself — I gather from the tenor of your letter — why our Schopenhauer esteems pain and trouble a great gift of fate, the δεύτεροσ πλοῦσ to the resigning of the will. You too have felt and lived through the enlightening, deeply quieting and settling power of pain. It is a time in which you can yourself try out the teaching of Schopenhauer. If the fourth book of his masterpiece now make on you an ugly disturbing downweighing impression, if it have not the power to uplift you, to carry you through outer violent grief to that chastened yet serene mood that comes over us as we listen to noble music, to that mood in which one feels the earthy shell to have dropped from one, — then I too will have no more of this philosophy. Only the deeply suffering can and may speak the final word on such matters. The rest of us standing in the current of things, only longing for that denial of the will as for the blessed isles, can not judge whether the solace of such philosophy is adequate to times of deep sorrow." [1]

And some three years later, Nietzsche invalided home from the hospital corps of the Prussian army writes to this same friend at the front: "This morning brought me the happiest surprise and a relief from much inquietude and anxiety — your letter. . . . Everything that you write affects me deeply, above all the sincere earnest tone with which you speak of this test by fire of our common philosophy of life. I too have been through a like experience, for me too these months have proved a time in which my beliefs have shown themselves deep-rooted. One can die with them; that means much more than saying, one can live by them." [2]

One may die by the light of Schopenhauerian principles! To die by them — the taunt comes from an older Nietzsche — is all that one can do with them. But by this later time, dying, voluntary dying, dying with the breath still left in the body — all this has lost its charm for Nietzsche. He is now all for living; for more than living, for fighting; for conquering; for, if need be, killing.

"One who like me," he writes in these later days,

[1] Gesammelte Briefe, p. 61.
[2] Ibid., p. 170.

" has long busied himself with curious interest in thinking out pessimism to its bitter end . . . has probably in this very pursuit — without precisely having willed it — turned his eyes toward the opposite ideal: toward the ideal of the most domineering, the most living, the most aggressive of men, toward him who has not merely reconciled and adjusted himself to things as they are and have been; but who wants more of them, just as they are and have been — more in all eternity, crying insatiably *da capo* not to his own life only, but to the whole scene and all the play."

The passage is not without a hint of Nietzsche's personal psychology. No doubt he loved contrast for the sake of contrast; no doubt he loved drama — particularly the dramatic conflict of ideas — for the play's sake; no doubt he loved paradox not a little for its noise. Yet it is not hard for the student to make out motives deeper than the personal, and more general, that impelled Nietzsche to turn his eyes from the ethics of self-sacrifice to the opposite ideal, to the ideal of " the most living, the most aggressive of men," to the ideal of the " Caesarian Conqueror."

No understanding of these motives can leave out of account the great scientific idea that had made its appearance in the nineteenth century — the idea of organic evolution. It is difficult to overestimate the suggestion that would lie in such an idea for one imbued with the thought of Schopenhauer. In its Darwinian form, the essential mechanism of evolution is seen to be a struggle, a war between race and race, between individual and individual. That such warfare is the necessary expression of the will to live, the most universal principle of that troubled phenomenon we call nature, Schopenhauer had indeed grasped, had insisted upon, had made the cornerstone of his theory of life. But then Schopenhauer had dwelt with equal insistence on the uselessness, the irrationality of the struggle. It was all cruel, then, nowhere benign, because nowhere directed toward an end. But now a purpose in the struggle is just what the evolutionary hypothesis seems to suggest. What if life's pitiless cruelty were justified as the indispensable means to a supreme end — the end namely of producing a being higher than any of those that take part in it? By the selection of the fittest, would not this warfare result in the production of the superior? And if the superior could be produced only at the cost of the inferior, is there not in this sacrifice something more than wanton and irrational cruelty?

It is little wonder that one already impressed

with the " self-contradiction " involved in a will not to live should seize upon this suggestion. " I bring you a goal," cries Zarathustra. And this goal he calls the " Uebermensch."

" I preach to you the Superman. Man is something to be overcome. What have you done to overcome him?

" All things before you have produced something beyond themselves, and would you be the ebb of this great flood? Would you rather go back to the animal than overcome man?

" What is the ape to man? A jest or a bitter shame. And just that shall man be to the Superman, a jest or a bitter shame.

" You have traveled the way from worm to man, and much in you is still worm. . . .

" Lo, I preach to you the Superman.

" The Superman is the meaning of the earth."

To produce the higher race! that is " the meaning of the earth," the meaning that Schopenhauer had missed, that only one coming after Darwin could have seized; a meaning that does not mask the cruelty of life, yet takes from it its tragedy — the tragedy of senseless casual pain.

But now that we have found the goal, we may also define the worth of life and its duties. In deducing these we meet the most astonishing " Um-werthung aller Werthe," the complete inversion of those notions of worth which we dwellers in Chris-tendom have inherited. " I sit," says Zarathustra, " with old shattered tables of the law around me — and with new tables, too, half made out." We ap-proach an understanding of Nietzsche's meaning when he wrote that God and man dies of pity. For if with him we make whatever promotes progress toward the superman our good, whatever retards it our evil, then must it not be that a pity which spares the weak for pity's sake is the very vice, the moral disease, which makes for decadence? Is not pity the anodyne of those who despair of life, and is not hope in the future necessarily cruel?

Before we who are of necessity touched with modernity react against a doctrine so little in accord with our profession of self-sacrifice, it would be well to ask ourselves how seriously we take this our profession. Is the quality of mercy indeed never strained for us? For example, are we citizens of a young and prosperous country eager to throw open its doors to the unhappy dregs of outworn lands and exhausted civilizations? For this would be the char-itable thing to do. How many are prepared to en-courage the mentally unsound or physically diseased to propagate? Yet pity must deny itself something if it would condemn misfortune to wed loneliness.

To be sure one expects at this point to hear of " the deeper pity "; to be told that such deeper pity must let some perish in their misery that more may not be made wretched. Even so, we have passed from the doctrine of the supremacy of charity to the theory of " the greatest happiness to the greatest number." Already we must occasionally cry with Nietzsche, " Be hard! " and must at moments understand his phrase, " The will not-to-help may be higher than the sympathy that springs to aid."

And we might carry our criticism of sympathy a step further. What sanction has the formula " the greatest happiness to the greatest number " ? Obviously, the sanction of the approval of the greatest number; it is the complete expression of the egoism of the mob. But egoism for egoism, is there anything to recommend the ideal of the mob as against that of the exceptional being? Surely, if we make progress our guide, those who have done the most to bring about modern conditions are just those whom the mob has condemned and suppressed as working against its welfare. Socrates was poisoned, Jesus crucified, Caesar assassinated, Bruno burned, Napoleon isolated, for their crimes. It makes little difference whether the crime was against the state, the priestly tradition, the republic, the church, the nations; the power to punish in each case came from the masses. Each of these conquerors was and had to be a pitiless egoist, hesitating not at all to overturn the world of his day for the sake of his own ideal. Looking back on these historic figures, one is tempted to say that the glory of the world abides in its criminals, those lonely men, those egoists.

If I have included the gentle figure of Jesus in a list of the conquerors, it is not because Nietzsche would regard him as one who had made for the world's progress, however much he may have contributed to its history. Nietzsche would, however, include the founder of the gospel of love among the master egoists. Of course, modernity will cry paradox! "Granted," it will say, "granted he brought a sword into the world, was it not an enormous pity for the humanity that was to be that moved him to destroy the world that was, and with it, himself?"

Nietzsche's handling of this paradox is one of the significant movements of his thought. To understand it we must go back a little. It is not the question of the personality of Jesus, of the motives that were clearly present to his own consciousness that Nietzsche would discuss. In general, he is completely indifferent to the kind of evidence furnished by self-analysis respecting the motives of conduct and the ground of opinion. Even those whose powers of analysis might be supposed to give them a right to speak — the great philosophers and lovers of truth — are to Nietzsche deceivers or self-deceived. " What tempts me to look upon all philosophers half with mistrust, half with amusement is not that one discovers again and again what innocents they are, how often and how easily mistaken and misled, not, in a word, their prattle and childishness. It is rather that, in spite of the great and virtuous noise made by the whole company the moment the question of truth is even remotely touched on, they do not deal ingenuously with us. They all pose as believing that they have arrived at their own opinions by the self-development of a cool pure and divinely impassible dialectic (in contrast with the mystics of all shades, who, honest fools, *will* speak of Inspiration). At bottom, however, it is some idea loved at first sight, most frequently some heart's desire made abstract and well refined that they defend with reasons found for the purpose. Advocates denying the name, cunning special pleaders for their prejudices, they christen these *The Truth.*"

If then the lover of truth cannot tell the truth about himself, if the cool thinker is unable to reveal the grounds of his thought, how much less can the man of heart tell what is at the bottom of his heart, the man of passion tell where his deepest passion lies? It remains for Nietzsche to make good these short-comings.

And Nietzsche makes them good in a way that lacks neither simplicity nor decision. He lays it down that there is one motive to which all others reduce, and to which everything that lives instinctively reacts. This motive is not the mere desire to preserve oneself, the desire that many have supposed sufficient to explain even the phenomenon of evolution. It goes beyond self-defense to strive after the maximum of aggression. Nietzsche calls it " der Wille zur Macht " —the Lust of Power. It is this that makes the world dance, that makes the brute prepare the way for man, that drives man to produce the superman. It is consequently this that compels the thinker to his thought, the meek to his resignation, the crucified to his cross.

" I am not of those of whom one asks ' why? ' " Nietzsche has once written. If you cannot accept his assurance that the deepest spring of conduct is the will to conquer, then accept the contrary doctrine: Nietzsche is prepared to trust his insight that you do this because the contrary doctrine is just the one *you* need to work out your own scheme of conquest, — as a wolf may on occasion sincerely prefer the pelt of a lamb to his own natural coat.

It is to the lust of power in men's hearts that the gospel of the crucified one appeals! The paradox is perhaps most completely worked out in Nietzsche's " Genealogie der Moral." Here history is made to reveal a long conflict between two contradictory estimates of worth. For the one standard a contrast exists between high morals and low; for the other, between holiness and sin. The code of ethics based on the first of these contrasts embodies, as the etymology of its terms indicates, the aristocratic conception of worth. " High morals " are simply the manners of the upper, the ruling class; " low morals," the habits of the underlings. This standard of valuation is accepted by the high and low alike of a race in its youth and strength. The second standard defining the opposition between good and evil is an invention of the miserable and oppressed; it is their reaction against their conquerors, the expression of their resentment. It can only become dominant in decadent races; its triumph in Christianity is evidence that the modern world has sunk to the ideals of the lowly — that is to say, of the low.

If we place these two codes side by side, we realize how completely the acceptance of either demands the "Umwerthung aller Werthe" acknowledged by the other. The highest worth in the aristocratic morality is the pride of strength; the great wickedness to the lowly moralist is just this same pride of strength. The great virtue of the slave-morality is humility; to the aristocratic taste this humility is abject. Of the history of the warfare between the two, Nietzsche gives a sufficiently dramatic account. Characteristic is his picture of the triumph of the slaves:

"All that has been accomplished on the earth against the higher orders is as nothing compared with what the Jews have done: the Jews, that priest-led people that finally contrived to have satisfaction of its enemies by a complete upsetting of all their ethical standards, in other words, by an act of intellectual revenge. It was the Jews who with inexorable logic dared to deny the aristocratic equation (good = lofty = powerful = beautiful = fortunate = god-favored) and who with bottomless hatred — the hatred born of impotence — set their teeth in a formula: to wit, ' only the wretched are the good; only the poor, the weak, the lowly are the good; the suffering, the sick, the unlovely are indeed the only servants of God and the only ones blessed of God — while you, O ye high and mighty, you are in all eternity the men of sin, of violence, of lust, the insatiable, the Godless, and you shall be in all eternity the unblessed, the accursed, the damned! ' . . . With the Jews begins the slave-morality, that morality which has a struggle of two thousand years behind it, one which we fail to note to-day, just because — it is victorious."

The master is made to accept the slave-morality, the tyrant is made afraid! Our English poet Browning has given a picture of this moment in history which surpasses even Nietzsche's in vividness. The man-forsaken, cowering yonder in his self-less humility — tempts the tyrant to wring from him one gesture of rebellion, one word that suggests pride of self. In vain! The slave's arm of defense is just non-resistance, just a mimicry of non-entity.

> When sudden . . . how think ye the end?
> Did I say " without friend " ?
> Say rather, from marge to blue marge
> The whole sky grew his targe
> With the sun's self for visible boss,
> While an Arm ran across
> Which the earth heaved beneath like a breast
> Where the wretch was safe prest!
> Do you see? Just my vengeance complete,
> The man sprang to his feet,
> Stood erect, caught at God's skirts, and prayed!
> — So, *I* was afraid!

But the psychology of this fear of the Lord that is the beginning of decadence? How is the tyrant to be made to accept the " Sklavenmoral," to respect, even to imitate humility and to call it holy? Well, the slave has on his side two things that make for success: superior numbers and superior cunning. For " only those who have need of cunning," Nietzsche writes, " acquire it." And the strong has one vulnerable point — his superstition. It is this point that the instinct of slave-hatred has found; with cunning and with numbers it has managed to inculcate a belief in the God of Pity, to overthrow the aristocratic appreciation of high and low, to substitute for it a morality of the miserable that sets up the distinction between holiness and sin. It is the denial of the will to conquer implied by such a standard of conduct that makes modernity decadent, that unfits it to produce the superman. No wonder Nietzsche should have claimed the gratitude of higher men for his glad tidings, the God of Pity is dead!

In passing beyond the morality of decadence, every suggestion of a plan of life that might be substituted for it, must come from the past: the young races not yet fallen into decrepitude give us our models of the heroic. We cannot however turn the clock back, we cannot repeat their acts today without becoming such anachronisms as a Cervantes could make laughter of. It may be however that our own institutions, foremost of which is the well-organized state, leave ample room for the heroism that prepares the way for the superman.

"Where the state ends — there begins the man who is not superfluous. . . .

"Where the state ends — Look, my brothers! Do you not see the rainbow and the bridges that lead to the Superman?"

Where the state ends! only there does Nietzsche's interest begin. But would he have the state end much nearer its beginning; yes, before its beginning; would he return to the condition that has no social, no political organization? Perhaps — it is hard to say; but it is not necessary that one advocate anarchy in order that one should prepare a field for that great struggle of man against man out of which are to emerge the victors, the fathers of the superman.

Huxley suggests another solution. For him too where the state ends a new struggle begins. The state assures security of life, and of this security is born a new desire — the *aviditas vitae,* let us say the desire for the maximum of life measured in terms of power and enjoyment. With this struggle born of the *aviditas vitae*, begins Nietzsche's theory of ethical values. Here indeed there can be no question of unselfishness, of self-sacrifice for another. Within this domain the meaning of good and bad stands out with perfect clearness.

" What is good? " Nietzsche asks. " All that heightens in man the feeling of power, the desire for power, power itself.

" What is bad? All that comes from weakness.

" What is happiness? The feeling that our strength grows, that an obstacle is overcome.

" Not contentment, but more power; not universal peace, but war; not virtue, but forcefulness.

" The weak and ineffective must go under; first principle of *our* love of humanity. And one should even lend one's hand to this end.

" What is more harmful than any vice? Pity for the condition of the ineffectives and weak — Christianity."

Yet one must not imagine that this pitiless struggle of which is to be born the man of tomorrow is gloomy and hate-inspired. On the contrary it is joyous, and gives scope for a much nobler love than that which is pitiful. I know of no institution of modern life that so nearly realizes Nietzsche's idea of this struggle together with the virtues it engenders, as does that of sport among gentlemen. Here one plays to win, and to spare one's opponent or to be spared by him merely mars sport. Yet one does not hate one's opponent, but loves him for his good sportsmanship. Only, this love, this friendship among strong men must not weaken the arm, must not soften the will; if it do, it destroys itself and is returned with contempt. We do not hate men because we fear them, Nietzsche makes it out, but just because we do not fear them. The hatred that leads one to shun one's kind is born of disdain. Life that has for its joy the joy of battle, for its reward the sense of strength that grows with its exercise, for its delight the love of brother warriors, a brother that can give and take death generously! It is only the many too many, weakly looking on and trembling before the spectacle of a strength they fear and hate, that have no joy of life and cry, " Let there be peace."

I would willingly describe this Homeric scene more in detail, consider the part that certain heroes, the warrior, the artist, the philosopher, play in it. But we must sweep on to larger issues, for there is a question that must have occurred to everyone as our description of the Nietzschian battle has advanced. It is the old question, Cui bono! We fight, suppose we win? Little Peterkin, who was surely brought up on Schopenhauer, is there to ask, What good has come of it? A little power more or less, what does it matter? Our brief hour is still a brief hour, our atomic selves cannot greatly swell, what after all is the use of fighting when we cannot befool ourselves as to the nature of the spoils?

For answer, we might point once more to the Superman. For him we kill pity in our hearts; for him, and not for spoils, is the battle fought. Surely the conqueror is conquered and his winnings cannot warm a grave. It is for the sake of them that come after that the costly struggle is maintained. Every fighter should know this; it should fire his heart and give him courage to be hard. " Higher than the love of thy nearest stands the love of those most remote from thee, thine offspring, the far future man. Higher than the love of thy kind is for me the love of a Shadow. This Shadow that runs before thee is more beautiful than thou; why dost thou not give him thy flesh and thy bones? "

But this Superman? Can things stop with him? Is he really a goal? Or only a transition, a bridge to the super-superman? Has evolution really changed the situation that Schopenhauer depicts? In the endless flux can one find a purpose that abides?

This phrase — the endless flux — brings us to one of the strangest phases of Nietzsche's doctrine.

One who, with Schopenhauer, has deeply questioned the evidence of purpose, the harmony of purposes in this world of ours, one who has groped in the night of things for that which might inspire one's will to live has perhaps been caught by the great idea of evolution, has perhaps cried with Nietzsche, " I will live and struggle for to-morrow." Then, to such an one, the old questioning spirit returns as it is bound to return to men who think. The morrow of to-morrow looms up before him; the eternal flux of to-morrows stretches itself out and loses itself in a vague " Whither? "

If now this one turn to Nietzsche for an answer, he receives one certainly; but, surely, a mocking one!

" I preach," cries Nietzsche, " the Wiederkunft."

One day Zarathustra and his Dwarf come to a certain portal.

" Look on this portal, Dwarf. It has two faces; two ways come together here which no man has traveled to the end.

" This long road back of us measures an eternity. And that long road before us — that is another eternity.

" They are opposed, these two ways; they meet each other head-on and it is here at this portal that they come together. The name of this portal is written over it; it is the ' *Now*.'

"But if one were to follow one of these roads further, and always further, — thinkest thou, Dwarf, they would always be opposed?

"Look upon this '*Now*'! From this portal there runs a long way back; behind us lies an eternity.

"Must not all things that can come to pass already have passed along this road? Must not everything that can happen already have happened and run its course?

"And if all things already have come to pass, what thinkest thou, Dwarf, of this '*Now*'? Must not this portal have been here before? And are not all things in such wise fast knotted together that this '*Now*' drags with it all things to come? That, consequently, it drags itself back again?

"For what of all things can come to pass, must they not again pass along this endless road that stretches before us?

"And this slow spider crawling in the moon-light; aye, and this moonlight, and I and thou in the portal whispering together, whispering of eternal things, must we not all of us have been before?

"And must we not return again and again along that long road — must we not eternally return?

"So spake he, and always lower and lower;

for he was afraid of his thoughts — and after-thoughts! "

Surely Nietzsche is mocking us with his Wieder-kunft, — with his doctrine of the eternal returning of things! What! he teaches that the struggle has a goal, and that goal is just — tomorrow? Then, when bewildered by the vision of the infinite stretch of tomorrows we turn to him for explanation, he tells us that the stream is not even infinite but like ancient Ocean " flows in upon itself."

" Tied to the wheel of things," India said we were, " therefore, let us give up."

" Tied to the wheel of things," Nietzsche agrees we are, " therefore, let us keep on."

" Courage is the best of them that kill. Courage kills even pity. Now, pity is the deep abyss: deep as one sees into life, just so deep does one see into pain.

" But courage is the best of them that kill; courage that lays hold on things; courage puts even Death to death, for it says to life: ' War das das Leben? Wohlan! Noch einmal! ' "

Noch einmal! To make one ready to cry *da capo* to life, that is the test of a philosophy! Nietzsche's doctrine of the Wiederkunft has no scientific importance, but this fact is itself unimportant. It makes little difference whether the River Ocean flows in upon itself, or flows endlessly on, or falls at last into Hades. The important thing is that worth and happiness lie in playing the game of life as experience reveals it to us, no matter what that game may be.

" Thy will be my will, O Nature," cried the Stoic Emperor. Is this will the will to conquer, is it the will to produce the higher type, is it the will to flow, is it the will wheel-like to turn in saecula saeculorum — the word of life is " That also will I "; the word of sickness and death is, " That will I not."

There is enough of the dramatic for such as have a taste that way in the circumstance that just this lonely, pain-wracked, finally brain-sick man should have begun his philosophy with the phrase: " God is dead of pity for men," and should have concluded it with that other: " War das das Leben? Wohlan! Noch einmal! "

VIII

PRAGMATISM

PRAGMATISM

Nothing could be easier, you would say, than to distinguish the things man has made from those he has merely stumbled upon and found. The suns and their satellites, with the laws of their turning; the earth, with its seas and continents and the ways of its winds and weather — surely no man took thought on these things to make them. Whereas, from the first bit of flint chipped to serve a human need to all our world has now to show of instruments of power and works of art we have a record of human ideals wrought in material, while man, surrounded by his handiwork, has come to live more and more under laws of his own making.

Aristotle thought the difference between products of nature and works of art so plain that he need not pause to explain it. The years that have passed since then have developed no better mind than Aristotle's, no keener wit than Plato's, but they have brought us a wealth of experience — of an experience at once enlightening and disillusioning, until

> Jetzt sind wir so klug und witzig
> Es verblutet uns das Herz.

We are no longer sure of very much, and among the things we are most doubtful about is just this distinction between what man has made and what he has found. To prove this, no one need go further afield than just to consider himself. Surely I may say of myself, my character, my private life that it is man-made, for am not I the man that made it? It expresses all my ideals so far as I could realize them, and never would it have been just what it is had I not moulded it that way. And yet, who among us has not sat up of nights with that strange being he calls himself, and wondered however he came to bring so uncompanionable a companion home with him and where the devil he found him? Ernst Mach tells an amusing anecdote at his own expense. One day he was mounting the steps of a bus when he noticed at the other end of the aisle a man's face peering into his. He had no more than asked himself " Where have I seen that degenerate looking pedagogue before? " — when he discovered he was looking into a mirror.

And who, wearying of this sorry companion, has not tried to change him for a better, only to find himself after a longer or shorter while with the same old fellow at his elbow — a trifle more set in his ways, perhaps, but otherwise little altered? Of the sadder sort of autobiographies I should put the

Journal Intime of Henri-Frédéric Amiel easily first. Not from pain or poverty, not from the malice of other men nor any disgrace of outer fortune did he suffer, but just from the being that was himself. "From the beginning," he writes in 1858, "I have been a dreamer fearing to act — in love with perfection and as incapable of renouncing her demands as of meeting them. In short, a mind of wide vision and a character of no strength; curious to feel all that is to be felt, unfit for any action." "Here," comments his friend, Edmond Scherer, "we have Amiel's cross. He wanted — he wanted to want — to will, and will-power was wanting in him. He cursed the inner spell that was on him, but he could not shake it off. After each attempt to break it he fell back into himself again, more bewildered, more weary and bruised than ever. In the waging of these combats the years wore on, until the moment was near when Amiel would have to acknowledge to himself that the circle was definitely closed behind him." Would you say that Amiel had made his destiny or found it? Would you say that any of us is of his own workmanship, or does our life slowly unfold itself to us as to Oedipus his fate?

What is thus suggested by self-examination is confirmed by the study of other lives. The friend whose wayward course has made your affection anxious for him — can you, with the best will in the world, change him from himself? Some, out of bitterness of their experience, have said it would be easier to repeal the law of gravitation than in any way to alter human destiny. Others to be sure are more sanguine, and will not give up seeking a way so long as there is a will to save. But whether, even when they appear to succeed, it is not rather their patience that is rewarded by being allowed to live long enough to witness what would have come about without any of their doing, or whether character is more truly a thing made by human effort than a thing found and unfolded to our observation — respecting these matters there is divergence of opinion.

Now, confidence in our ability to tell what we have made from what we have found once shaken, there is no saying how far our questioning mind may carry us. No saying, I mean, in the case of any individual man — for it is easy enough to tell the general history of this doubt and uncertainty. It reaches all the way from those who think that back of all apparent creating by finite beings there is a Nature with its laws that was never made, but can only little by little be made out. Let us call those who think in this way " Realists." Historic uncertainty then reaches all the way from the realists to those who think that heaven, the earth, and all that in them is, have no reality save as they are the thought and work of finite minds. We will call these thinkers " Idealists." From realist to idealist and back again, through all intermediate phases, the dialectic of history swings; but it does not merely mark time therefore, it also measures progress. It is of one moment — I think a rather interesting moment — of this progress that I would speak in due order. Let this, then, be my prologue — and so to the tale.

In 1907, William James wrote of the philosophy to which he had devoted the last ten or twelve years: " I fully expect to see the pragmatist view," so he called this philosophy, " run through the classic stages of a theory's career. First, you know, a new theory is attacked as absurd; then, it is admitted to be true, but obvious and insignificant; finally, it is seen to be so important that its adversaries claim they themselves discovered it. Our doctrine of truth is at present in the first of these three stages, with symptoms of the second stage having begun in certain quarters."

Looking back over the years that have lapsed since this was written, I cannot say that James's prophecy as to the future of pragmatism has been fulfilled; but that the world, at least the world in which I have lived, has lost its first sense of the absurdity of pragmatism is undoubtedly true. No one was more bitten than I with this first feeling of the absurd, unless it was some other of my kind among those who gathered of an evening in 1896 to listen to a reading of James's now famous little essay on " The Will to Believe " — the essay which, so far as James was concerned, opened the campaign for pragmatism. James had written the paper that winter as a lecture to be delivered before the Philosophical Clubs of Yale and Brown Universities, and I cannot recall what the occasion was that brought a small number of us graduate students at Harvard together to hear it re-read; but I do recall that we were very much bewildered and not a little shocked by the reading.

Not all, I dare say, who afterwards read this " Will to Believe " will have experienced any such shock and bewilderment, nor will many have felt what we found so upsetting in a bit of writing that was, as writing, certainly, altogether delightful. But you must know that this particular gathering was made up of students who had been brought up in that theory of truth which I have called the realistic, and their habitual attitude toward truth was such that they held their truth the truer the more they were its discoverers and the less they had had to do with the making of it.

There were, to begin with, the laboratory men. Now, a laboratory is a school of the most rigid discipline — a discipline whose first principle is " keep yourself out of your experiment." I think you will understand what I mean by this when I say that a scrupulous experimenter about to take conclusive readings in a matter that promises to be of some value to science will, if possible, get another observer ignorant of their import to take these readings for him, lest something of his own excitement and anxiety corrupt his very touch, sight and hearing, and warp his result to his will. And, what was this James was defending — a " Will to Believe "? No wonder some wag of the lot dubbed it " The Will to Make Believe " ! And what was this again James was saying — " For purposes of discovery . . . indifference is to be less highly recommended, and science would be far less advanced than she is if the passionate desires of individuals to get their own faiths confirmed had been kept out of the game. . . . On the other hand, if you want an absolute duffer in an investigation, you must, after all, take the man who has no interest whatever in its results: he is the warranted incapable, the positive fool." Had James addressed a gathering of the Sons of St. Patrick, in the sense of demonstrating to them that the Pope of Rome was the Beast mentioned in Revelations, he might have called forth a noisier response, but none less sympathetic than ours.

One who would invite a man to bring his enthusiasms, his likings and dislikings, in short, any will of his other than the will to persevere, into a laboratory with him would naturally not forbid him to keep all this equipment by him in whatever pursuit of truth he might engage, whether of history, economics, morals or religion. And just as James shocked the realist spirit of that little Harvard gathering of a score of years ago, so have his writings fallen afoul of realism wherever they have been read — and perhaps few writers on philosophy have been more widely read than William James. This is to have made enemies indeed, for the genius of realism, the spirit of the seeker who would find what he might find and call it truth, naked, unclothed upon with garments of human interpretation, has sometime breathed in every science and every art.

Take the realistic historian now — but you will doubtless know this character better if I show him to you, and the effect he produces upon other temperaments, than if I merely describe him as a type.

PRAGMATISM

Among the most entertaining of the reviews that Anatole France contributed to " Le Temps," in the late 80's and early 90's, is one that he devotes to a work " tout à fait solide et puissant " of Louis Bourdeau, " L'Histoire et les Historiens, essai critique " — a critical essay on history considered as an objective science — " in which," as France remarks, " M. Bourdeau puts works on history in a class with fables and Mother Goose tales.

" ' History,' says M. Bourdeau, ' is not and cannot be a science.' The reasons he gives for this have not failed to make an impression on my mind, and perhaps there is a special reason why they should impress me — the sum of which is that I had tried to point out these reasons before he did. I had thrown out suggestions of them flippantly and in a spirit of badinage ten years ago in a little book of mine called the ' Crime of Sylvestre Bonnard.' I set no store by them then, but, now that I see they are worth something, I am in haste to claim them.

" ' In the first place,' I said in this little book, — ' In the first place, what is history? History is the written presentation of past events. But what is an event? Is it any fact whatever? No, sir. It is a noteworthy fact. Now, how is the historian to judge whether a fact is noteworthy or not? He judges according to his taste and caprice, follows his own idea, in short, proceeds after the manner of an artist. For facts do not of their own accord divide themselves into historical facts and non-historical facts. Again, a fact is something extremely complex. Does the historian represent facts in all their complexity? No, that is impossible. He will represent them stripped of the greater part of their detail, consequently truncated, mutilated, different from what they were. As to the interrelation of these facts, the less said of that the better. If a so-called historic fact is brought about (which is possible) by one or more non-historic facts — and for that very reason unknown — how can the historian establish a relation between these facts? '

" These, if I am not mistaken, are the fundamental ideas upon which M. Louis Bourdeau rests his right to refuse to history any scientific value. . . .

" Indulgent minds find a way to get along with the treacheries of history. This muse is false, they think, but she no longer deceives us when we have found out that she is deceiving us. Constant doubt shall be our kind of certitude, they say. Prudently, we will go our way from error to error toward a relative kind of truth, for even a lie is some kind of a truth. . . .

" But as for M. Bourdeau, he does not wish to be deceived even knowingly, and he absolutely repudiates history. He drives her from his door as deceitful, shameless, dissolute, having sold herself to the powerful, a courtesan in the pay of kings, an enemy of the people, wanton and false."

So far, the picture of non-objective history in all its ugliness — history as it has been written in the past. But now the history of the future, objective history, realistic history — ah, that will be quite another story. It is Bourdeau who speaks: "The historians of the future will have for their first task the gathering and interpreting of statistical data concerning the common events of life. The activity of thought always expresses itself in acts, and the only way to take account of these is, after having classified them under definite functions, to set them down at the moment of their happening, to count them under given conditions of population, of time and place, then to compare these results whether simultaneous or successive, to note the variations of the function and to make the inductions that they warrant. Thus, and only thus, may we some day know what the multitudes that make up humanity are doing.

"This is the way we must write history from now on, not only in the young countries which, like Australia, Canada, La Plata, are founded under new conditions, but even in the old societies of Europe that, like the others, hope to work out for themselves an ideal order of labor, of peace and of liberty. For one who has reached our point of advancement, any other way of studying history is inexact and childish. A reform is coming, and will either be made by the historians or in spite of them. The age of literary historiography is about to close; that of scientific history about to open. When it shall be able to reconstruct for us the life of a people in the way we have indicated, we shall see that no story can offer so much of interest, of instruction and of grandeur."

I do not know that every one is bound to share Bourdeau's enthusiasm for statistical history. Perhaps some will hope with France that they may not be spared to read history written in this way, and will solace themselves the meanwhile with their Thucydides and Herodotus. But at least, all will have caught the martial tread of realism resounding through these passages.

In the laboratory sciences the objective spirit sits as a strong man in his castle, impregnable, unattackable. There we see him dreaming dreams of conquest, the fair domain of history, in which we may include economics, seems ready to fall to his bow and spear for the world's endless betterment. And what lies beyond? Lands that are the fairest, richest, most desired of all; and yet which will take all his daring, all his courage, all his steadfastness and an undying enthusiasm to make his own. They are the lands of morals and religion.

I like those chapters of history that tell how the spirit of the experimenter sets out to conquer the realms that have so long been ruled by masters with whom he can have no sympathy — tradition, coming out of the vague mists of the past; superstition, born of human ignorance; mysticism, inarticulate, ecstatic, offering reasons for itself that are reasons only to those who ask for none. To win all this for objectivity, for the kingdom of the kind of truth that believes only because the experiment says so, the experiment that any unbeliever may repeat for himself and abide by the result — this is surely a brave adventure, and whether they meet victory or defeat one cannot refuse one's enthusiasm to those who have had courage to make it.

Of those who set forth in this way, I should call David Hume the father. Would you, for example, know what is right and what is wrong? Then turn not to inspired writings, but travel widely through the civilizations of different countries and different times and seek as you would seek any other historical fact, first, what people *called* good and what they *called* bad. Then, if underlying the vast contradictions of historic precept you find nevertheless an agreement in the purpose these precepts, set in their native settings, served, why, then, you will have arrived at the only meaning good and bad can have.

Or, would you know whether this is God's world or no? Turn not to reputed miracles, and indulge not in idle dreams of another world in which the faulty humanity and utter finiteness of this one will have found its supplement and correction; but, take just the order and purpose of this world as your best experience reveals it to you. It may be that this seeking will leave you dark, puzzled, uncertain; but better the unrest of judgment suspended than the dream-like peace of faith unfounded.

> It fortifies my soul to know
> That, though I perish, truth is so.

wrote Arthur Clough. And, again, he has written:

> To spend uncounted years of pain,
> Again, again and yet again,
> In working out in heart and brain
> The problem of our being here;
> To gather facts from far and near,
> Upon the mind to hold them clear,
> And, knowing more may yet appear,
> Unto one's latest breath to fear
> The premature result to draw —
> Is this the object, end and law,
> And purpose of our being here?

PRAGMATISM

Over these verses Clough has written: " Perchè pensa? Pensando s'invecchia."

Why think, indeed, when thinking leaves one old —so old, so cold, so sadly wise? That thinking — the realist's way of thinking — does leave one in melancholy mood may be no objection to thinking in this way; but it may not be ignored as a fact of history. Realism's hymn of triumph is written by the best of its poets and the most sincere of its prophets — Leconte de Lisle. One does not attempt to translate a Leconte de Lisle, but the thought of the final verses of his poem on the Southland may be put in some such way as this —

Man, if with heart full of joy or bitterness
Thou go at noonday through these radiant fields —
Flee! Nature is empty and the sun consumes;
Nothing here is alive, nothing sad, nothing joyous.

But if having put tears behind thee and laughter
Thou be turned to forgetfulness of this troubled world,
No longer knowing how to pardon nor how to curse,
And would taste a last sad volupté —

Come! The sun speaks to thee a glorious language;
Lose thyself in its implacable flame
And return slow-footed to the vile city of men,
Thy soul seven times steeped in divine nothingness.

It is like that. This wondering in a world we did not make and cannot change, in which all our creating is illusory — a chance trivial expression of what the world has made us — with no other purpose in our wandering but

> For to admire and for to see,
> For to be'old this world so wide.

— why yes, the fulness of such experience comes as near as can be to bringing us to a seven-fold sense of the *néant divin*.

Well, when a man's philosophy has turned bitter to his tongue and hangs heavy on his heart, there are three things he may do. He may abide by the consequences of his philosophy, and seeing no fault in the premises accept the conclusion with all valiance. Or, he may rebel against all logic and reason and trust that sympathies and antipathies are safer guides to truth than any evidence could be. Or, finally, he may examine the premises anew. It is, I must confess, only to the last — to the reasoners and critics who go patiently to work to re-examine old beliefs — that I lend a respectful ear. But I do not know that I can begin an account of the backward swing from such extreme realism as I have pictured to such extreme idealism as I can tell only part of before I close, better than by letting the mere spirit of unreasoning revolt against this selfless objectivity express itself.

With an exquisite insight into the psychology of those he calls " Wir Gelehrten," and with no care for the truth or error of the ways of the objective spirit, Nietzsche registers his revolt against all this spirit stands for. " However gratefully we may still welcome the objective spirit," he writes in his " Jenseits von Gut und Böse," " in the end we must learn to put some caution into our gratitude and some restraint on the enthusiasm with which selfless-ness and impersonality of mind have come to be extolled as ends in themselves, as an emancipation and an enlightenment. The objective man who no longer curses or upbraids, the ideal scholar in whom the scientific instinct after a thousand whole or half failures has at last come to full growth and blossom-ing, is surely the most precious tool there is; but his proper place is in the hands of a stronger man than he is. We say he is an instrument — he is a mirror, he is no end in himself. The objective man is in-deed a mirror. Accustomed to subject himself to all that is to be known, without any other pleasure than such as the knowing, the mirroring gives, he waits till something comes his way, then spreads him-self delicately before it so that the light foot-steps and ghostly passing of spirit things may not be lost to his surface and integument. What there is of a person still left in him seems to him accidental, often arbitrary, oftener still disturbing; so much has what was his very self become a medium through which pass and in which are reflected foreign forms and happenings. If he tries to think about himself at all, it is an effort for him and more often than not a failure. He changes easily; he tries to grasp his own needs, and only then is he clumsy and awkward. Perhaps it is his health that bothers him, or the petty pent-up character of wife or friend, or the lack of companions and companionship. Oh, yes, he tries to think out what is the matter with him. No use! Already his thought has swept on to the more general case, and tomorrow he will know as little as he did yesterday what's to be done about it. He has lost serious interest in himself, time spent on himself is wasted. He is cheerful, not for want of things to worry about, but for want of fingers and hands to lay hold on his trouble. His way of taking whatever turns up, his sunny unconstrained hospitality to anything that comes along, his way of wishing everybody well, his dangerous indifference to the difference between yes and no — ah, how often he has to pay for these his virtues! And, as just a man, he is too often taken for the caput mortuum of these virtues. Would you have him love or hate — I mean love or hate as God, women and brutes understand love and hate — why, he will do the best he can and give what he can. But no one should be disappointed if this is not much; if just here he shows himself ungenuine, unattached, unreliable — rotten. His love is thought out, his hates are trumped up and rather a *tour de force,* little side issues and exaggerations. He is only genuine when nothing prevents him from being objective. His mirroring and everlastingly even soul can no longer say " yes," no longer say " no." It imposes nothing on anything, neither does it upset anything. It says with Leibnitz, " Je ne méprise presque rien."

If in this passage Nietzsche reveals his delicate antipathy for a character we had all been taught to worship, in others he shows himself a pragmatist before that word had been heard of. The philosopher for him is no wanderer of the seas, accepting what shores he comes upon whether they smile on him or frown. For Nietzsche, the philosopher is a Caesarian conqueror who has his way with truth, and truth is such a thing as a strong man may have his way with.

But, " I am not of those of whom one asks ' why? ' " Nietzsche has somewhere written, and this is so true that I can use him for no more than a vehement example of spleen. If I am to enter upon the path of a more or less reasoned reaction against that objectivity we have all sometime held sacred, I must turn to those of whom one can ask "why?" And, notably, to William James.

Now, if I do turn to James to ask him "why?" — Why is not the realist, with all his sad heroism and resigned courage, the noblest and best that man has imagined? — he answers, or I take him to, Because realism is a philosophy of little faith! Faith it is that makes worlds, realistic science has only the wit to acknowledge and the strength to suffer what faith has wrought. Bold to endure, it is timid to change, and a world in the making needs its makers, needs its poets and actors more than it needs audience or spectator. At the bottom of the realist's brave heart lurks an abiding fear — the fear of making a fool of himself. But a world in the making like a battle in the fighting cries out for fools and the foolhardy. Faith risks to the point of folly, and because all making anew is a colossal risk, let us have colossal faith.

Here, if I am not mistaken, you have the principal difference between the realism that went before and the pragmatism that came after. The faith which the builders rejected is become the head of the corner. For there are such things, the pragmatist contends, as faiths that realize themselves, beliefs that come true only because they are firmly held and courageously acted upon, hopes that would never have been fulfilled had not he who held them gone ahead in the confident expectation that they would be fulfilled. Take, James would have you, just that familiar class of questions of fact, "questions concerning personal relations, states of mind between one man and another. *Do you like me or not?* — for example. Whether you do or not depends, in countless instances, on whether I meet you half way, am willing to assume that you must like me, and show you trust and expectation. The previous faith on my part in your liking's existence is in such cases what makes your liking come. But if I stand aloof, and refuse to budge an inch until I have objective evidence, until you shall have done something apt [as the realists say] *ad extorquendum assensum meum*, ten to one your liking never comes. How many women's hearts are vanquished by the mere sanguine insistence of some man that they *must* love him! He will not consent to the hypothesis that they cannot. The desire for a certain kind of truth here brings about that special truth's existence, and so it is in innumerable cases of other sorts. Who gains promotions, boons, appointments, but the man in whose life they are seen to play the part of live hypotheses, who discounts them, sacrifices other things for their sake before they have come, and takes risks for them in advance? His faith acts on the powers above him as a claim, and creates its own verification."

These be but trifling affairs of commonplace life if you will, but the imagination sweeps easily on from the relation of man and man to all that man's work which is done shoulder to shoulder. "A social organism," James goes on, "of any sort whatever, large or small, is what it is because each member proceeds to his own duty with a trust that the other members will simultaneously do theirs. Wherever a desired result is achieved by the co-operation of many independent persons, its existence as a fact is a pure consequence of the precursive faith in one another of those immediately concerned. A government, an army, a commercial system, a ship, a college, an athletic team, all exist on this condition, without which not only is nothing achieved, but nothing is even attempted. A whole train of passengers (individually brave enough) will be looted by a few highwaymen, simply because the latter can count on one another, while each passenger fears that if he makes a movement of resistance, he will be shot before anyone else backs him up. If we believed that the whole car-full would rise at once with us, we should each severally rise, and train robbing would never even be attempted."

Have you ever, O patient reader, in the heat of a political campaign for what you thought were better things met with that cool chilling intelligence that hastens to warn you against trying to change human nature? As it was in the beginning it is now and ever shall be, gangs without end. Amen! And he is right, this unduped and undupable intelligence is right — but on one condition only: The world will always be as it was at the beginning if it is exclusively inhabited by unduped and undupable intelligences — by realists, in short. Or, have you ever tried to refresh your tired soul with what the Germans have written of Realpolitik? If so, you will already know a great deal of what pragmatism is *not*. It is not a philosophy of the " what never has been never can be " temper of mind.

" There are cases," James puts it, " where a fact cannot come at all unless a preliminary faith exists in its coming. *And where faith in a fact can help create the fact*, that would be an insane logic which would say [with Huxley] that faith running ahead of scientific evidence is the ' lowest kind of immorality into which a thinking being may fall.' . . ."

I am afraid there is about the pragmatist something of that dangerous citizen who will not hesitate on occasion to grasp this sorry scheme of things entire and shatter it to bits, full of the faith that it can be remoulded closer to the heart's desire.

"But now," James returns to his argument, "these are all childish human cases, and have nothing to do with the great cosmical matters, like the question of religious faith. Let us then pass on to that. . . .

"To most of us religion comes in a way that makes a veto on our active faith illogical. The more perfect and more eternal aspect of the universe is represented in our religions as having a personal form. The universe is no longer a mere *It* to us, but a *Thou*, if we are religious; and any relation that may be possible from person to person might be possible here. For instance, although in one sense we are passive portions of the universe, in another we show a curious autonomy, as if we were small active centers on our own account. We feel, too, as if the appeal of religion to us were made to our own active good-will, as if evidence might be forever withheld unless we met the hypothesis half way. To take a trivial illustration: just as a man who, in a company of gentlemen made no advances, asked a warrant for every concession, and believed no one's word without proof, would cut himself off by such churlishness from all the social rewards that a more trusting spirit would earn, — so here, one who should shut himself up in snarling logicality and try to make the gods extort his recognition willy-nilly, or not get it at all, might cut himself off forever from his only opportunity of making the gods' acquaintance. This feeling . . . that by obstinately believing that there are gods . . . we are doing the universe the deepest service we can, seems part of the being and essence of the religious hypothesis."

I do not lay this passage before you as an example of clear thinking and cogent reasoning. Who does not find it baffling, elusive, leading to no kind of action, must have a mind differently constituted from mine or from any with which I am more intimately acquainted. It is, if you please, the groping of a faith that feels it has a right to exist, but does not know as yet what is right for it to do. All of which is most unpragmatic — not at all practical. But perhaps this very quality, this manner of James's of feeling his way through the dark *en tâtonnant*, with his heart's courage for his only light, is what most endears him to our age. We sit with Zarathustra midst shattered tables of the law, and our awkward fingers cannot grave new ones hurriedly. We fumble, we hesitate, we begin again.

We fumble, we hesitate, but we *do*, if we are idealists, begin again.

Now, one of the new things we have tried is just
this manner of meeting the universe half way in the
matter of religious faith.   And this trial has been
no interchange of philosophical abstractions; but a
struggle of very living men.   To tell about it will
perhaps illustrate better than anything else the appeal pragmatism made to some and the offense it
gave to others.

We have all known, though doubtless our fathers
knew him better, that studious theologian who, as
proof of a devout life's industry, left behind him
a Testament worn to something like its elemental
dust.   He was a realist in temperament, and sought
God and God's meaning in documents as an historian might seek to reconstruct some character of
the past from the archives.   He was supplemented
in his labors by learned indefatigable searchers of
other remains of the past from whose ruins they
sought to bring corroborative testimony.   He was
opposed only by other students who had pored over
their Testaments with equal devotion, if to opposite
purpose, and by other archaeologists who had
searched the ruins with equal pains, if with other
result.   But protagonist and antagonist alike of the

Christianity into which we were born were realists. Neither dreamt that the existence or non-existence, the benevolence or cruelty, the oneness or manyness of God were matters with which his personal wishes and strivings, his finite wantings and not wantings could have anything to do. If you had suggested to either that perhaps God was still in the making and that those who would know Him must strain their eyes toward the future, not keep them fixed on the past — it is a question which would have been first to put you down as an impious fellow and a blasphemer.

How different from all this is the spirit of that recent movement within the Christian church that is generally called Modernism! "Defined and condemned in the encyclical *Pascendi*," writes J. Bourdeau, in 1907, "modernism continues to fill the reviews and the periodicals, even those that ordinarily treat of matters profane. This internal crisis of Catholicism, this new attempt to reconcile the church with the times, aimed at internal reform, not at schism. It was destined to end in the excommunication or interdiction of some of its more refractory spirits and in the submission of almost all. And yet, by those who shared its hopes, modernism is not looked upon as the bed of a torrent from now on to be dry; it runs like an underground river, and some day, perhaps, will come to the surface again with sufficient force to sweep away the dikes."

Well, this modernism which M. Bourdeau, in his little volume, "Pragmatisme et Modernisme," brackets with pragmatism as being of the same temper, is, like all other modernities, not very new. We associate it with such names as Father Tyrrel, in England; l'Abbé Loisy, in France; the senator and novelist Fogazzaro, in Italy, and if the matter has interested us, with a host of other writers no less distinguished. But it is really of the essence of Newman, and goes back to Pascal. For "The heart," Pascal has said, "has its reasons that the reason does not understand." It was to these reasons that Newman listened, and offers us again in his "Grammar of Assent," and it is these reasons that modernism would have to be the only ones on which Christianity can be safely founded.

But what are they, these reasons, and what does this voice of the heart say? Its first clear utterance is negative. It does not care who wrote the various books of the Scriptures, or what corroborative or contradictory evidence those who study the documents and monuments of the past may come upon. "Higher critics," so far from being its enemies, are welcome participants in its cause. As little does it cling to the literal sense of the various dogmatic interpretations the Church has from time to time put upon the sacred writings. Would you know, for example, whether there is a Real Presence? Modernism would answer: The Eucharist is indeed meaningless unless there be a Real Presence; but whether Christ is really there for you or not depends on you alone. And the like of other dogmas.

Yet it would appear that history, sacred, ecclesiastical, or profane, is no dead letter to the modernist. He is intensely conscious and amply studious of the past. Nor will he, if I make him out, permit its episodes to be treated as symbols, parables and allegories. No, the past tells the story of a great religious truth in the making. If you ask him what Christianity is, he will tell you it isn't, it never has been, it never will be any definitely finished thing; but for him it is the best guide to living that he with all his devotion and all his thought can make it. The modernists are Christians because they are heirs to, and imbued with the spirit of Christianity, as they are not inspired of the Buddha or of Confucius. Yes, they are devout Catholics because they can work better at the making of a religion in the atmosphere of their ancestral church than in any other air. Religion to them is to aid in the way best suited to their temperaments and traditions in the evolution of religion; for them Christianity is in process, and we are the potters that mould it, not the explorers that discover it.

Well, J. Bourdeau is not wrong; modernism and pragmatism are indeed of like temper and children of the same age — an age of troubled outlook, but of brave if chastened hope. The contrast between the realistic theologian with his ancient texts, documents, monuments, and the idealistic theologian who turns to the past not for authority but for guidance, not for facts but for a sense of tendency and direction — this contrast is not unlike that other one pragmatism has brought about between "Natural Religion" and what I may call "Human Religion." Natural religion sought in the order of nature evidence of its designer, of a thoughtful purpose back of or in it, the same spirit that a naturalist might hunt for the tracks of a mastodon or follow the wanderings of a glacier. For the humanist, the purpose of nature is a thing in the making, and we are here to help make it. It will turn out as our finite efforts form it — good or bad, as we are good or bad; wise or not, as we are. The practical message of "Human Religion" is pretty much that with which James closes his little essay, "Is Life Worth Living?" "Be not afraid of life. Believe that life *is* worth living and your belief helps create the fact. The ' scientific proof ' that you are right may not be clear before the day of judgment (or some stage of being which that expression may serve to symbolize) is reached. But the faithful fighters of this hour, or the beings that then and there will represent them, may then turn to the fainthearted who here decline to go on with words like those with which Henry IV. greeted the tardy Crillon after a great victory had been gained: 'Hang yourself, brave Crillon! we fought at Arques, and you were not there.' "

I have tried to show pragmatism as a moment in the swing of thought from realism to idealism, and how for it the most vital, that is to say, the moral and religious aspects of our world are things to work and fight for, to make and to mould, not just to find and come across. Its god is indeed a god of battles, and we are his soldiers on whom his victory depends. But as I view this battle, it is not to be fought out in heart throes and outpourings of sentiment. These may indeed change and better human relationships; but it must not be forgotten that human relationships exist in a physical universe that is older than they, and promises to outlast them. Now, just the physics of things show a strong tendency to be amoral and atheistic. " You all know the picture of the last state of the universe which evolutionary science foresees. I cannot state it better than in Mr. Balfour's words: ' The energies of our system will decay, the glory of the sun will be dimmed, and the earth, tideless and inert, will no longer tolerate the race which has for a moment disturbed its solitude. Man will go down into the pit and all his thoughts will perish. The uneasy consciousness which in this obscure corner has for a brief space broken the contented silence of the universe will be at rest. Matter will know itself no longer. " Imperishable monuments " and " immortal deeds," death itself, and love stronger than death, will be as if they had not been. Nor will anything that is be better or worse for all that the labor, genius, devotion, and suffering of man have striven through countless ages to effect.'

" That," comments James, " is the sting of it, that in the vast drifting of the cosmic weather, though many a jeweled shore appears, and many an enchanted cloud-bank floats away, long lingering ere it be dissolved — even as ours now lingers for our joy — yet, when these transient products are gone, nothing, absolutely *nothing* remains to represent those particular qualities, those elements of preciousness which they may have enshrined. Dead and gone are they, gone utterly from the very sphere and room of being. Without an echo; without a memory; without an influence on aught that they may come after to make it care for similar ideals." [1]

Has not, then, realism the last word in this argument and does not the rolling mechanism of things have its way with us in the end — since it compasses not only our death, but the collapse of the very theatre in which our little lives have played themselves out?

No, I should say, this is not the moral of the tale, though there is a moral to the tale. " Knowledge," writes Francis Bacon, in his " Novum Organum," " knowledge and human power are synonymous." So are human impotence and human ignorance synonymous. The child that dips a cup of water from the fountain is subduing nature's mechanism to its needs. It is only a question of how great is our knowledge if we would know how great is our power.

We die, our world dies, only because we know no better, have thought of no way of preventing; but knowledge and human power are indeed synonymous, and I know of no end to either. But, as for those of us bound to die before we have learned how not to, and as for our children whose world may well vanish before they have thought of a way

[1] Pragmatism, p. 104.

of saving it, we have always this solace — that we
know we are facing the only way salvation can come
from when our face is toward science. " For nature," says Bacon, with his queer crooked smile, —
" nature is only subdued by submission."

IX

PROGRESS

PROGRESS

For much there is that is fair in the lives of the Typees. Dwelling on that enchanted island of the Pacific, their lines are cast in pleasant places. The asperities which civilization seems rather to have aggravated than smoothed do not roughen their way. Their existence is passed in the midst of tropical plenty, on which their numbers, few and hot on the increase, make light demand. They toil not to cover what nature has conceived in innocence, and spin but lightly to adorn what nature has fashioned fair. Little thought do they take on their housing. " There are few villages," Melville tells us, " the houses stand here and there in the shadow of groves or are scattered along the banks of the winding stream; their bamboo sides and their gleaming white thatch forming a beautiful contrast to the perpetual verdure in which they are embowered. There are no roads of any kind in the valley; nothing but a labyrinth of foot paths twisting and turning without end." Yet the morals of these people do not seem to have been so far below our standards as their benighted condition might lead us to expect. " There seemed," says Melville, " to be no rogues of any sort in Typee. In the darkest nights the natives slept securely with all their worldly wealth around them, in houses the doors of which were never fastened. The disquieting thought of theft and assassination never disturbed them. Each islander reposed beneath his own palmetto thatching, or sat under his own breadfruit tree, with none to molest or alarm him. There was not a padlock in the valley."

I had gone so far in one of my readings of Melville, and was beginning to wonder in the back of my head what a Typee introduced into our civilization could find to say of us half as pleasant as the things their guest had noted of them, when I recalled that another had long ago put the like question to himself when he was in much better position to answer it. It was when the New World was very much newer than it is now, that Villegaignon landed in a country he surnamed Antarctic France, where dwelt a people of cannibals the very counterpart (as I judge) of our friends the Typees. "Three of these people," the Sieur de Montaigne records, "were at Rouen in the reign of our late King, Charles the Ninth, who talked with them a great while. They were showed our fashions, our pomp, and the form of a fair city; afterwards some demanded their advice, and would needs know of them what things of note and admirable they had observed amongst us. They answered three things," . . . of which Montaigne seems particularly impressed with this one: " They had perceived [they said] there were men

" Those nations seem therefore so barbarous unto me because they have received very little fashion from human wit, and are yet near their original naturality. The laws of nature do yet command them which are but little bastardized by ours, and that with such purity as I am sometimes grieved the knowledge of it came not sooner to light, what time there were men that, better than we, could have judged of it. I am sorry Lycurgus and Plato had it not; for me seemeth that what in these nations we see by experience doth not only exceed all the pictures wherewith licentious poesy hath proudly embellished the Golden Age, but also the conception and desire of philosophy. . . . It is a nation, would I answer Plato, that hath no kind of traffic, no knowledge of letters, no name of magistrate nor of politic priority, no use of service, of riches or of poverty, no occupation but idle, no respect of kindred but common, no apparel but natural, no measuring of lands, no use of wine, corn or metal. . . . The very words that import lying, falsehood, treason, dissimulation, covetousness, envy, detraction and pardon were never heard of amongst them. How dissonant would Plato find his imaginary commonwealth from this perfection?

Hos natura modos primum dedit. "

PROGRESS

I had thought to begin a sound philosophical account of the nature of progress with a picture, not, if I could help it, unsympathetic, of man's condition before he had felt its benefits. The plan would recommend itself to any philosopher as suitable and convenient to its purpose, yet here am I well beyond the beginning of my discourse, still lingering with the cannibals, and, what is worse, sensible that I have not been diligent to uncover the many causes there must be for rejoicing that we are not as they were. Not that there is any difficulty in pointing to the host of things we can do which they could not. We have only to mount in one of our winged ships and look down on the simple Typee rubbing two sticks together for their spark, to see in all the distance that lies between us the like of what Prometheus scaled Heaven for. But what in all this is there to rejoice over?

It is singular how many have asked this question and found no answer, or have answered — Nothing. I do not cite the licentious poets Montaigne refers to as having invented a Golden Age and feigned a happy condition of man before progress had spoiled the world for him; although these are many, and if their wisdom is not of the philosopher's kind, yet is it all the closer to that " ancient wisdom of childhood " a wise man does well to keep near him.

But even learned academies have thought the question not beyond their interest and study. In 1749, the Academy of Dijon set for the prize competition of the following year the question, " Whether the progress of the arts and sciences had contributed to the purification of life? " The prize was won by J.-J. Rousseau. His little essay, generally known as the " Discours sur les Sciences et les Arts," worked on the thought of its time as seldom so casual a thing. " One cannot," Jean-Jacques wrote then, " one cannot reflect on the ways of life without finding pleasure in recalling the image of its first simplicity. That was a fair shore, bedecked by only Nature's hand, toward which our eyes are ever turning back regretfully as we watch it fade in the distance."

There may be, nay, I think there must be, a meaning and a moral to this disgust of the enlightened here and now, this longing for a life not all " sicklied o'er with the pale cast of thought." But the interpretations of this feeling we most commonly meet with are not I hope to be taken very seriously, for if they are, there is no counsel for us but one of despair. Thus, whatever could come of the lament for the good old days, the golden days, before science had done this or that to cloud our first innocence? No history written in such ancient times but that it can recall times still more ancient when things went better with the sons of the gods because then they knew less. And it is still open to any one — traveler, philosopher, poet — to draw what picture he will of far away lands wherein, for that nobody wanted very much, everybody found all he wanted. The subject of this sketch may vary from Diogenes snarling in his tub to a Typee girl dancing in her flowers; from the desert to which the Christian cenobites withdrew to Tasso's bosky places, where, before that vain word Onore had mingled its grief with love,

> Sedean pastēri e ninfe,
> Meschiando alle parole
> Vezzi e susurri, ed ai susurri i baci
> Strettamente tenaci . . .

But of all this, nothing is serious, nothing sincere, — of all those who lament the past not one would take the first step toward it, so little is it in man's nature to retreat. Or if anyone would, yet what could he do, save drag his own sadness into the desert with him? As for the world, it must even go on with its science, though it be but the science of hurting itself.

Wherefore, no less futile than regret for a past we cannot recover, is fear for a future we cannot avert. It is natural that certain conditions arising out of the progress of science should make gentle souls anxious for what is to come. Science is power, and as no man can commit the sins he is impotent to commit, there is a certain safeguard for innocence in ignorance. Only after having eaten of the Tree of Knowledge did our first parents come to mourn outside the gates. No shepherds and shepherdesses conceived the iniquity of Babel's tower, and Egypt and great Babylon were of no children's dreaming. Yet must man go on gathering unto himself knowledge with all its power for harm and no warning gesture of the fearful can stay him. Our only comfort can be that however great a power for harm science may bring, it ought to enhance in equal measure the power for good, — did we but know what good and evil were.

Did we but know good and evil! In the suggestion that perhaps we do not, in the suspicion that this is just the knowledge to which science does not help us, — yes, in the fear that it is science itself which throws doubt on ethical standards — is, I conceive, a motive for deprecating the progress of science more serious than the others, and more sincere. Science is, indeed, endlessly critical; no authority of tradition or of general acceptance imposes upon it; nothing for it is finished, nothing fixed; and to those to whom all goodness is in danger the moment one asks, What is good? science may well seem a dangerous growth, — unhallowed in its origin, curiosity; damnable in its outcome, unrest. And yet if as we assume science must progress, stayed neither by regret for the past nor by fear for the future, then must its questioning spirit invade every realm of opinion, examine the most sacred of beliefs, look into the very meaning of good and evil.

For this reason we did well, I conceive, to begin a consideration of progress with some account of the skeptics. Science itself cannot quarrel with those who meet its advances with the question, What is the good of you? But it can only begin its answer by asking another, What do you take to be good?

What do you take to be good? Evidently there cannot be two minds, one of which points to the advance of civilization with every confidence that it means the world's betterment, the other conceiving that men may grow wiser and none the better for that, unless *the good* is understood by them in different senses. What are these two meanings tangled in the single word, — *the good?*

It is this question that Immanuel Kant has studied with peculiar care and thoughtfulness in his

Morality no doubt first presents itself to most of us as a set of laws or maxims of conduct to follow which is virtue. These laws we may think of as delivered unto man in God's own voice, and carved upon tables of stone. Or, if our image of their origin and authority be not so definite, we may still find moral peace in the thought that what words the still small voice of conscience whispers to us are no less God's words. They are what Antigone took them to be —

> The immutable unwritten law of Heaven.
> They were not born today or yesterday;
> They die not, and none knoweth whence they sprang.

If many have been unable to keep the sweet moral confidence of childhood until the end, it is because riper experience has not confirmed to them Antigone's premises, nor mature reflection born out her conclusions. Do they *not* die, these unwritten laws: are new ones, indeed, never born? For a little searching we may find that not a precept marks a virtue for one people at one time, but that elsewhere or elsewhen its ordinance is taken to be vicious. And conversely, we do not have to travel far to find vice turning into virtue. Antigone's own people are not so remote from us as the Mingrelians and Topinamboues; we owe them much that we prize most in our culture, and would be proud to match them in more ways than one. And yet, consider their admiration in the way of a man, which, if it was any one, was surely the Wise Ulysses. Now, if there are any two principles of Christian morals more firmly planted in our souls than others, they are the maxims, Be truthful, and, Be kind. But was Ulysses truthful? was Ulysses kind? To leave for one's unconquered enemies a wooden horse as it were a parting token may be an innocent enough thing to do, however pagan. But to make of this wooden horse a disguised troop ship is not within the strict letter of truthfulness; and to sally forth therefrom to slay your quondam foes while they sleep in the security of your peace does not show a kindly spirit. Yet it does not appear that the Greek gods resented any more than did the Greek people Ulysses' cruel craft: all of which would lead one to suspect that the unwritten law of peoples, if indeed it come from Heaven, must come from only that part of it which is directly overhead at the time.

But let time and place be never so circumscribed, and men never so in accord as to their moral maxims, are these maxims at least consistent with one another? Does one bid us be truthful? — then another bids us be kind! But how in this vale of

was fond of calling "loyalty," the devotion of my will to the will of another. I am aware that not just *any* other-will, whosesoever it may be, is contemplated by moralists as a fit object of loyalty's devotion. The Other to whom my will should bow, if I would be moral, is generally conceived to be more numerous than I (e.g. the majority), or more inclusive (the family, the state, the cause), or in some sense higher (God). In short, the Other-will is taken to be, in one way or another, an Over-will, and moralists may differ widely as to which one of several conceivable Over-wills should be recognized as the Absolute. But for the purpose of this discussion, one illustration of moral loyalty is as good as another, for the difficulty that morality has found in making good its claim to have laid hold on the absolute good lies not, I conceive, in deciding *which* Other-will is sovereign, but in convincing a man that he ought to acknowledge as sovereign *any* other will than his own. One who is told that it is not good for him to remain captain of his soul is bound to ask, Why not? It is morality's way of dealing with this *why* that I would consider in an example which, for being simple, loses nothing that I can think essential to the issue.

In Thomas Hobbes's "Leviathan," one finds an

account, clear, legalistic, unsentimental, of the meaning of duty interpreted as the obligation of your will and mine to bow to a Sovereign-will. The title-page of the first edition (1651) of this work bears the image of a man of heroic size whose body is made up of little men. The little men stand for you and me, the big man is Leviathan. The story of the generation of the living giant made up of living men is in this wise:

" Nature it seems hath made men so equal . . . as though there be found one man manifestly stronger in body or quicker in mind than another, yet when all is reckoned together the difference between man and man is not so considerable as that one man can therefore claim to himself any benefit to which another man may not pretend as well as he. . . . From this equality of ability arises equality of hope in attaining of our ends. And therefore if any two men desire the same thing, they become enemies, and in the way to their end . . . endeavor to destroy or subdue one another. . . . From this diffidence of one another, there is no way for any man to secure himself so reasonable as anticipation; that is, by force or wiles to master the persons of all the men he can, so long till he see no other power great enough to endanger him. . . .

" Hereby is manifest that during the time men live without a common power to keep them all in awe, they are in that condition which is called war, and such a war as is of all against all. . . . In such condition there is no place for industry, because the fruit thereof is uncertain, . . . no arts, no letters, no society, and, what is worst of all, continued fear and danger of violent death, and the life of man solitary, poor, nasty, brutish and short. . . .

" And consequently, it is a precept, or general rule of reason, *that every man ought to endeavor peace, as far as he has hope of obtaining it; and when he cannot obtain it, that he may seek and use all helps and advantages of war.* . . . From this fundamental law of nature, by which men are commended to endeavor peace, is derived this second law; *that a man be willing when others are so too, as far forth as for peace and defence of himself he shall think it necessary, to lay down this right to all things, and be contented with so much liberty against other men as he would allow other men against himself.*"

Thus " the final cause, end, or design of men, who naturally love liberty and dominion over others, in the introduction of restraint upon themselves in which we see them live in commonwealths, is the foresight of their own preservation, and of a more contented life thereby; that is to say, of getting themselves out from the condition of war, which is necessarily consequent to the natural passions of men when there is no visible power to keep them in awe and tie them by fear of punishment to the performance of their covenants."

Now "the only way to erect such a common power . . . is to confer all their power and strength upon one man or upon an assembly of men that may reduce all their wills . . . unto one will, . . . which is as much as to say, to appoint one man or an assembly of men to bear their person, and every one to own and acknowledge himself to be author of whatsoever he that so beareth their person shall act . . . in those things which concern the common peace and safety; and therein submit their wills every one to his will, and their judgments to his judgment. . . . This done, the multitude so united in one person is called a Commonwealth, in Latin, Civitas. This is the generation of that great Leviathan, or rather, to speak more reverently, of that *mortal god* to which we owe under immortal God our peace and defence."

Seldom has the "generation" of an Absolute been so clearly set forth. We do not suppose, any more than Hobbes himself did, that this word "generation" has any historical significance. Men never lived in the state of nature here defined, they never foregathered to reason out in this way the advisability of organizing themselves into commonwealths. Instead of " generation," read, if you will, " justification," i.e., the justification in reason for the commonwealth's existence and dominion. Then observe that not only does this great loyalist (the whole Leviathan is one of the loyalist documents of the Civil Wars) — not only does he demand a reason for the loyal faith that is in him, but in the development of this reason it turns out that the absolute *is not another will at all*, but only one's own will thoughtfully dealing with others to win for itself a " more contented life."

Now of course it is an absurdity to try to give a reason why any will whatever should be taken for absolute and expect to keep it so; for the very function of this reason is to show what more ultimate end is served by acknowledging this will as master. But if we do follow Hobbes's reason for bowing as deep as we do bow to Leviathan, this reason is that our own deepest desire — or what Hobbes takes to be such — is thereby best served. " For it is," says he, " a voluntary act; and of the voluntary acts of every man, the object is some good to himself."

Why then, that morality which promised to give us a meaning of the good that would enable us to understand how the progress of science with its hypothetical goods might let us stray from or even lead us away from *the* good, has turned out to be itself offering us a hypothetical good, *to be itself an effort of science,* — the science of many wills meeting in presence of but a single world. And this I take to be the fate, not only of Hobbes's but of all moralities: differ as they may respecting that Other-will they take to be absolute, they all alike recommend a sacrifice of my will to another will, not indeed for the sacrifice' sake, nor yet for that other will's sake when all is said, but that my own will may find " a more contented life thereby."

Most of us have let our thoughts respecting the good of life stop with the acceptance of those moral goods that the opinion of our time takes to be absolute. These standard objects of loyalty, the state, the hearth, the cause, we serve with devotion and to them make our sacrifice. It is natural we should look with distrust, even with hostility, upon those who have let their thought go further and have asked, How in serving these Other-wills is our own deeper desire the better fulfilled? And yet, if our analysis is so far correct, this is the most intelligent, the most dignified of questions; for no historic morality has really meant to present itself as a system of sacrifices with no corresponding satisfactions.

But if we ask of the current morality of loyalty, What is the greater contentment bought by each of us at the price of the sacrifices we make in loyalty's name? we come upon serious matters for reflection. There have been those who maintain that current morality cannot meet the demands of intelligence, and as there are two ways in which in buying a thing for a price one may drive an unprofitable bargain, so there are two critics of current morality. The one thinks the price morality asks too high; the other esteems the thing bought of no value. Let me call the one the *Reforming Moralist;* the other the *Amoralist.*

Now the reward morality holds out to all who make sacrifice to it is some ideal of peace, whether it be peace on earth and good will among men, or that peace which passeth understanding. Our reforming moralist then holds fast to the ideal of peace as the deepest of human desires, but questions whether current morality in its uncritical acceptance of traditional loyalties has found the most intelligent, i.e., the least sacrificial way of peace. Thus if he is not blind to the citizen-peace that comes from living in Commonwealths to whose Over-will we particular men make our loyal sacrifices, neither will he accept such nationalism as refuses to sanction covenants of nation with nation to the establishment of their more peaceful, if less autonomous, relations. He sees in that group-will we call the national-will but an historic device for improving the conditions of private life. He sees nothing but unreformed, that is, atavistic and stupid morality in such nationalism as would make the autonomy of the state an end in itself to which private life must forever yield its contentment. There is a sense in which he would say with Remy de Gourmont —

" The life of nations, of groups, of individuals is one struggle against morality. Man pushes on toward liberty, and can accept only such discipline as assures him at the cost of temporary subjection a more agreeable and more complete exercise of this supreme good. All discipline that is not founded in liberty is caduque, and it is for this reason that civilization has always succeeded in surmounting systems of morals." [1]

But if our reforming moralist acknowledges the supreme value of peace and would only make the pursuit of it more intelligent, our amoralist denies that the human heart can ever rest in peace or even really wants to. Peace, if it were complete, would

---

[1] The meaning and value of " loyalty " is more fully discussed in Chap. X, on " Love and Loyalty."

mean stagnation, will-less apathy, that ennui of life Schopenhauer judges to be worse than any misery the war of aggressive wills can engender. In the Nietzschian man-of-might our amoralist sees his ideal, a will that knows no Over-will, acknowledges no loyalty, but whose motto is "Weltmacht oder Untergang." For him, life shall at least know nothing of ennui, no static stagnant peace, no Nirvana.

Thus if we approach in an historian's spirit the attempt to think out the world-desirable to make for which is to progress in the only sense the word can have, we find humanity divided between those who desire peace and those who want war.

On behalf of peace the moralist points not alone to the misery war brings to the vanquished, not alone to its cost to the victor and to the vanity of his ephemeral winnings; but to that utter loneliness which the war of all upon all makes the only lasting portion of each. A solitude of struggle, without one to cheer the effort, without one to share the joy (if joy it can then be called) of triumph — can any human heart endure, let alone desire war?

But the amoralist, full of the *certaminis gaudia,* turns in disgust from the hopeless state of the peaceful who having nothing more to fear can have nothing left to hope for. Our longing for peace is an illusion of certain moments of war-weariness, but a picture of eternal peace, stagnant, ambitionless, dead — and yet not dead enough — who could endure it, who could really desire peace?

Lonely ambition — peaceful acquiescence in a common lot! The history of human relations is a struggle, more often than not a compromise between these ideals. There is enough inspiring in each to make any man of understanding long for it, there is enough repulsive in each to turn any thoughtful soul against it. Wherefore the gruesome spectacle of world war is but the outer and visible sign of the struggle that goes on every silent moment within the heart of each, as the volcano is but the overt violence of long sullen rumblings that have gone before. And so things must last if and so long as we really want two irreconcilable ideals: compromise must follow makeshift, war must punctuate peace, world without end.

Into a world so distraught comes that child of God, that messenger of heaven, the modest philosopher. His cheerful gospel is that all men's ills are curable by taking thought, that men suffer only for their false philosophy. Now, of all philosophies none is so false as that which pretends one cannot have his penny and his cake. True it may be in the letter that I cannot keep a certain copper in my pocket and honestly entice a sweet-meat out of the baker's window. But I must be a sorry philosopher if I cannot keep all the potentiality of future enjoyment the penny stands for, and yet have all the actual satisfaction I happen for the moment to visualize in the form of cake. Or to put the thought in less poetic and more general terms, the heart that thinks itself torn by conflicting desires owes its plight to the failure of its imagination to realize that only the formulas in which it has so far expressed its desires are in contradiction; the desires themselves may well enough be reconciled in a larger world-view.

Take our present problem for example. It is impossible, you say, that I should deny the ambition to conquer for the sake of the love of my neighbor without killing what is most vital in myself. And it is equally impossible that I should give play to my ambition to conquer without losing my neighbor's love and living a lonely struggle. These things are indeed impossible in the world to which the imagination of the past has been fettered, — this little finite earth the fulness whereof is so easily emptied. If to have all that I can win of such meagre fulness is the only meaning I can give to ambition, either I must kill ambition and love my neighbor across a fence, or I must tear down the fence and kill my neighbor. But what if the fault of all this lay not with the darkness of reality, but with the blindness of untrained imagination? What if we could set before ambition a boundless prospect, so that never, far as conquest might reach, could it find cause to weep for lack of more to conquer? What if, in the very conquering of such a world, the gain of one, so far from being another's loss, were the equal spoil of all, yes, and a weapon forged to the hand of all for new victories? Wherefore *then* should ambition yield or love be denied?

But perhaps you will say, this *is* but an imagining and a dream. Our humdrum world, the only real one, offers no such object of ambition; and if it did, our nature, just human nature, is not such as could understand, still less be fascinated and inspired by it.

Does it sound ridiculous to say that our world *is* one that holds out just such a prospect to all who will but see? Aye, and that many a human eye has seen, and having seen remained single to this vision? I will call the promised land the Kingdom of Nature Subdued: I will call the vision the Vision of Science.

In the beginning, Man was Nature's creature and her plaything. Sometimes she seems to have fondled her toy and been good to it, given it pleasant places to dwell in and let the light of her countenance shine upon it. Those who think only of these rare moments may sing, O bella età dell' oro! O Paradise; O Paradise! They forget how rare were these moments and how capriciously bestowed. Elsewhere were many griefs of which man could not so much as guess the reason, and if he dared raise his questioning gaze to God he was mocked for his impotence and nothingness: "Where wast thou when I laid the foundation of the earth? declare, if thou hast understanding."

But need makes for perspicuity. Time passed, and some few caught a glimpse of the vision of science; caught it, widened it, brightened it and passed it on. Perhaps their lives were not very happy in a world where they were much alone; but it is easier to tell of their ostensible hardships than of their enthusiasms — who knows but that even they found here their compt? Time went on, and that Nature which had begun by being so cruel and capricious a mistress became through man's science more and more his slave. Human eyes were not so often turned to the gods in supplication. A Greek slave rang out to his fellows, "Why call ye upon the gods? Ye have hands? Wipe your own nose."

The earth yields; step by step death itself gives

ground; and shall we think of the stars only to fear them and to read our fate in them? Shall they forever whisper to us their old taunting questions: " Canst thou bind the sweet influences of the Pleiades, or loose the bands of Orion? Canst thou bring forth Mazaroth in his season? or canst thou guide Arcturus with his sons? Knowest thou the ordinances of heaven? canst thou set the dominion thereof on the earth? " — And shall we always answer, Alas!

But I am dreaming a dream. Is it though so ill a thing to dream, if one does not forget how to laugh the while? Yes, I know, the stars are rather big for our frail hands to play with even as all Nature once played with us. But how else am I to say that there is nothing in Nature that can forever resist the onward march of science? What else am I to say when the same master equations hold in heaven as on the earth, and Arcturus with all his sons is but a falling pebble painted large?

Let us dream then and laugh with Aesop at his frog. It is certain that neither our laughter nor our dreams can hurt our wise neighbor very much, and if we go the toilsome way toward the conquest we dream of, he or one that comes after may sometime look back on us and say, Yes, that was Progress. *The measure of man's coöperation with man in the conquest of nature measures progress.*

X

ROYCE ON LOVE AND LOYALTY

A Footnote in Illustration

ROYCE ON LOVE AND LOYALTY

[Something we had to say, in clarifying the thought of Kant, of a quality of human *love* that holds its object single and unique. And again, in estimating the part played by morality in the ideal of progress, we had occasion to remark the unwillingness of some to admit the finality of those sacrifices *loyalty* calls for.

These matters are not so simple but that history, in dealing with them, shows sharp discord where it does not uncover sheer confusion. The love that sets its heart on *one* has been held the highest; it has also been put the lowest of all loves. Loyalty that lives on sacrifice has been prized as an enduring condition of all worth; it has not escaped disparagement as a human makeshift. Above all, " love " and " loyalty " are so mixed in men's minds that, although any pair of lovers could tell a service of love from a servitude to loyalty, philosophers cannot always.

The brief discussion that follows seemed to the writer to illustrate a difficulty it may not have removed. He considered that it could not lack point for those who in foregoing passages on love and loyalty have found themselves more involved than enlightened. For the rest, it has seemed best to leave this " footnote " in the form and wording its original occasion inspired.[1]

One who like me has gone to Royce for wisdom now this long time and never come away empty, may yet live to know that some of his receivings are more his belongings than others. Thus, if it ever happen to me that I find my hold on the ' Absolute ' slackening and the thing slipping from me, I cannot think that even in that day I shall have forgotten two words I have heard. Love and loyalty, loyalty and love: this pair I expect will still be singing its burden in my soul after other things have left off singing there. But I hope that when this day comes I shall know better than I do now whether love and loyalty are two names for the same thing; or whether they are not the same, yet brothers and friends; or whether in the end they

[1] The paper on " Love and Loyalty " was written for the American Philosophical Association at its Philadelphia meeting in 1915. The occasion was peculiarly dedicated to Royce in honor of his sixtieth birthday. The author's thanks are due to Professor J. E. Creighton for his courteous permission to re-print from the Philosophical Review, XXV, 3, and from the volume " Papers in Honor of Josiah Royce, etc.," 1922.

are not rather enemies, of which one can survive
only if the other doesn't. Nor do I know, though
I should very much like to, how Royce himself
would answer these questions. Sometimes the words
fall in such close juxtaposition in his writings that
I wonder whether they do not express a single idea
whose peculiar quality is just unselfishness. But
again I bethink me that to be just unselfish is not
enough for an absolutist, if for anyone; that giving up can only be justified when it is a means of
acquiring; and I wonder what loyalty can have to
say for itself half as convincing as the things love
could point to. Until at last I find myself speculat-
ing whether if love had its perfect way with us there
would be any place left for loyalty in our lives, and
whether we could not look back on it then as on a
virtue happily outlived.

And this may be my matter in a nutshell — is not
loyalty a thing to be outlived, and is not that which
alone can enable us to live it down a love so perfect
it calls for no sacrifices? Some such thought has
long been with me, but if I am to lay my troubles
before you, it is time I put aside a language too rich
in sentimental associations and took up the idiom I
love best, that of cold and, if may be, mathematical
definition.

Any definition of loyalty that could have meaning for me must assume the existence of something many deny to have either existence or meaning, and which I shall call in my own way the mind of a group, or a group mind. The conception of a mind belonging to a group of beings each one of which has a mind of its own, yet such that the mind of the group is no more to be known from a study of its parts than is the mentality of Peter from the psychology of Paul, is a very old conception and perhaps for that reason supposed by some to be old-fashioned and out-worn. It is a mere analogy, they say, and a very thin one at that, to speak of a group of organisms as itself an organism; it is Plato, it is Cusanus, if you will, but it is not modern. Benedetto Croce even goes so far as to be polite about the matter. "The State," he writes, "is not an entity, but a fluid complex of various relations among individuals. It may be convenient to delimit this complex and to entify it for the sake of contrasting it with other complexes. No doubt this is so; but let us leave to the jurist the excogitation of this and the like distinctions — fictions, but opportune fictions — being careful not to call his work absurd. It is enough for us to be sure we do not forget that a fiction is a fiction."

To Royce the group mind is far from being a

fiction, though he may prefer to call it by some other name than group mind — maybe universal mind or universal will. But if to him it seems natural, as it does to me, to recognize group minds, while to Croce the entity is but a polite fiction to be pleasantly dismissed, there must be some lack of definition befogging our issue. Nor can I think of any way in which old issues can better be made clear than by recalling old images.

Aristotle would not have asked when and where do new *entities* appear, but where and when must we take account of new *forms*. Now matter was informed for Aristotle when the behavior of some class of beings was recognized to be predictable in terms of purpose. Thus earth, water, air and fire sought their proper places, one below, another above, and the others in between. But we remember how no sooner had these elements reached their proper places than, transformed by the sun's heat, they were no longer at home where they found themselves, but must needs seek their new homes anew. Thus homeward bound in opposite directions, they collided and became entangled, so that mixtures of the four appeared, which, as it proved, kept their proportions for a longer or shorter while ere they lost their equilibrium and fell apart again. Among these mixtures were vegetables and animals and men, but Aristotle is very far from defining this new class, organisms, in terms of the quantities of the elements that enter into their bodily composition. No, what they have in common and all they have in common is a new purpose, that of self-preservation (and, if we are to follow Aristotle rigorously, that of type-preservation). But why in this class of beings does a new form appear when there is nothing in any one of them but so much earth, so much water and so much of the rest? Because, I take it, in order that the purpose of the group may be realized, the purpose of each constituent of that group must be defeated: when the earth in us finds its way back to earth and our fire to fire, then we are no more. Which is the fundamental difference between us and them: if we win they lose; if they win we are done for. The whole has a purpose whose realization is only possible if the purposes defining the parts are given up for it.

I suppose Croce would say that nothing better could be offered in support of a modern fiction than an ancient fable; and I confess that I can think of nothing better fitted to set forth the complex problem of how beings of one mind can combine to form groups of another mind, than Aristotle's account of the way elements in the form of mechanism combine to produce a group with that other form, life.

Perhaps I can make out the connection between old and new ideas by a single example. I know of no fellow easier to get along with than your average Parisian: many a time have I sat at his board, looked in his eyes, listened to his amusing wit and wondered how the great-grandfather of my host could have been part of the Reign of Terror. And yet I suppose the Parisian of today is not very different from the Parisian of four generations ago, when groups of these same Parisians were ranging the streets of Paris crying, " A la lanterne! " However much it was in the character of the Pierre, Paul, Jean and Jacques Bonhomme of those old days to steer for home, their distributive tendency was contradicted by their collective tendency. A new form, a new entity had appeared; it was the spirit of the mob. It may be pleasant to call such new entities fictions; but it would be a most dangerous fiction to suppose pleasant men made pleasant mobs.

I must let this single illustration take the place of what might at some other time grow into a systematic account of the varieties of group minds that history and personal experience reveal to us. For my world is highly organized — groups within groups and groups within these in a way one might have learned at the feet of Nicolaus or by gathering one's history from Gierke's " Geschichte des Deutschen Rechts." But on this occasion, instead of going into all this literature and all this philosophy, let me come back to the matter of loyalty's worth. There would be no such thing as a demand for loyalty were there no call for a man to deny his wish for home — whether home be on earth or on high for him — for the sake of organizing himself into a group; which means, as we have seen, sacrificing his purpose for the group purpose. Now, what you think of the value of this sacrifice depends altogether on the esteem in which you hold group minds. If you can find some principle on which to estimate their dignity as something worth dying for in part or altogether, then loyalty may be the last word of virtue. But if you find that at their very best there is something rather primitive, sometimes amoeboid, sometimes tigerish about such minds, then you should seriously consider whether your biped soul owes anything more to this polypod entity than the entity owes to it. Merging oneself into something big may not be just the same as reaching for something high.

But I am not belittling loyalty. It is a great virtue so long as it understands itself to be making a virtue of necessity. Just so is it a great virtue to acquire equanimity in the face of death, in such wise

that not being able to invent a way of getting around
the thing one may accept it for the time being without disturbing oneself or one's friends more than
the episode calls for. Still, if I had some genius
to spend, I should rather contribute it to the sup-
pression of dying than to the cultivation of a cheerful manner in dying. So should I rather spend my
time, if it were worth while, in wearing away the
conditions that make loyalty necessary than in devel-
oping a spirit of loyalty. And so, or I mistake him,
would Royce; for I can not get over the impression
that for him, too, loyalty is but a half-way house
on the road to something better — which something
better is *love*.

It is with relief I find a definition of love can
be effected which makes no very heavy demands
upon one's sentimental experience; in fact, requires
no more in that way than a fair understanding of
the theory of substitutions. For the peculiar quality
Royce finds in the idea of love is that *love individuates*. This its quality is for him its virtue also and
its excellence, so that the more love individuates
the more is it love. We are far enough from the
days when a Plato could hold the love to be higher
that had detached itself from the individual and
attached itself to the quality, had forgotten the
beautiful being to think only of his beauty. For

Royce, love is not love unless it has succeeded in making its object irreplaceable.

Now I do not know whether this constitutes a complete definition of love. There is something hopeful about the suggestion that it may do so; for if no one has been able to say anything very articulate about love, neither has anyone said much that is intelligible about individuation. But certain difficulties occur to one. Is love the only thing that individuates? If there is such a thing as Platonic hate, which I suppose would be the sort of hate that hates the sin and not the sinner, why should there not be such a thing as a romantic hate whose object would be just the sinner and not his fault? Or may not a process of individuation go on, cold and impassible, untouched by either hate or love?

One day Flaubert took his disciple by the hand and led him into the secret places of art. The talent of the artist, he said, is a long patience spent in learning how to portray so that your portrayal leaves the object it offers just as individual as the thing is found. "When you pass a grocer sitting at his door, or a concierge smoking his pipe, or a stand of cabs, show me this grocer and this concierge, their pose, their physical appearance, suggesting also by the skill of your image all their moral nature in such wise that I do not confuse them with any other grocer or with any other concrierge. And make me see with a single stroke in what a certain cab horse is unlike fifty others following him or going before."

Why, then, besides love and hate, art too claims to be that which individuates — and not because, if we may believe a certain philosophically minded critic, art has borrowed anything of love or hate. This disciple of Flaubert, this Maupassant, carried out his master's teachings if ever an artist did, but there is that in his way of doing it which makes one feel that Anatole France's account of him is not altogether wanting: " He is the great painter of the human grimace. He paints without hate and without love, without anger and without pity — hardfisted peasants, drunken sailors, lost women, obscure clerks dried up in the air of the office, and all the humble folk whose humility is without beauty and without merit. All these grotesques and all these unfortunates he shows us so distinctly that we think we see them with our own eyes and find them more real than reality itself. He is a skillful artist who knows he has done all there is to do when he has given life to things. His indifference is as indifferent as nature."

I am not so very confident that all these claimants

to the right of individuating — love, hate, art —
are equal claimants. As for hate, some poverty of
experience may account for the fact that all I know
of this romantically valued emotion has sometime
been directed against persons unknown, whose manner of conducting themselves on the earth beneath
and in the waters under the earth showed nothing
more clearly than that they had forgotten the human
being and were utterly lost in loyalty. A hate of
such poor quality cannot well be said to individuate,
and it is certainly not any experience of my own
that would lead me to suppose romantic hate, as we
have imagined it, to be real. Respecting the im-
passibility of the creative artist, I am no less skepti-
cal, and so I think is France at bottom; for of this
same artist whose indifference is as indifferent as
nature, he says in another passage of the same appreciation that his hardened hero " is ashamed of
nothing but his large native kindliness, careful to
hide what is most exquisite in his soul."

No, I am not convinced that love has any rivals in
the art of individuating, and if not, then to call it
that which individuates is to define it completely.
But whether it is a deduction from this definition
or whether it is an independent element in a fuller
definition of love, it must be set down as an important fact about it that love wants the will and desire

of the beloved to prevail. It wants the will of another to prevail, and as the easiest and most obvious way of bringing about this result is to yield its own will, it has generally been supposed that love was less the art of individuating than the art of yielding. But this is just the mistake that has prevented love from taking its place among the more seriously meant categories of philosophy and realities of life; for this yielding disposition that might be supposed to make for peace in a republic of lovers is the very matter introducing trouble and perplexity there. It is the very matter that has made traditional Christianity less effective than it might have been, failing where it fails, not because there is anything better to be conceived than its gospel of love, but because it has supposed a good heart and convinced will was enough to bring about its kingdom.

Our two great experiments at loving — the love of man and woman and the love of one's neighbor — have been too much alike in this, that they both supposed love to be the sort of thing one could fall into and be done with. But it is clear this is not at all the way of the matter, and in our poor imaginings about the lovers' republic we have been too much guided by our imperfect experience of what our loves have been to think our way into what the

This, then, is thought's infinitely difficult task in the service of love, to analyze apparent desires until it has found the real want at the core of appearance, while the postulate on which alone the advent of the kingdom becomes possible is that thought may find our real wants not contradictory. The times are not without sign that Christianity as an ethics is coming to realize how very intellectual is the task it has set itself in trying to bring the kingdom of Christ's vision to be on earth. What Christianity most needs, writes Tennant, is a philosophy.

The brief time we allow ourselves for our utterances ought yet to prove ample for a person of industry and thrift to make himself thoroughly misunderstood; and I hope I have used it to no less purpose on this than on former occasions; but among the misunderstandings I would prevent, if I could, is that which would sum up the matter of my discourse as a defense of *individualism* against *collectivism*. Such an issue could only be meaningful for one to whom the collectivity was denied some sort of individuality which the " individual " enjoys. But I have tried to show that I could conceive no such difference between the mind of the part and the mind of the group. The group mind may be loved with the human love that individuates, as well as can the soul of a fellow-man; and no doubt one may love one's country as a mistress. But the difference between the love of equals and the love of constituents is plain. The latter sort of love can last only so long as its object endures, and as long as it lasts its sacrifices are incurable; for in a world that has conquered strife there would no longer be that contradiction between the will of a group and the will of its parts, which alone makes the group entity meaningful. Groups bound in mutual respect of each other and studying to preserve their parts irreplaceable *have no minds;* the entity born of struggle and calling for sacrifice has simply disappeared; where we had a group mind, we have now but an aggregate of minds, " a fluid complex of relations among individuals." But the love of equals can push on toward the ideal without destroying the very object of its devotion; it can go on searching the core of concord in the stupid appearance of discord until love has found a way to make loyalty a lost virtue and a group mind a thing that is no more.

RETROSPECT AND PROSPECT

WHEN I had gathered together the pages in which for a time I had been living with these men whose thought had been so real a thing to me, who one by one had said their word and left it to live or die according as men's hearts received it, I was as though suddenly and newly aware of the great modern city without pressing on my window-panes. Little by little its vast insistent presence seemed to push my whilom companions out of the room of being back to their places among the many silent dead. For indeed, I reflected, how few, how vanishingly small a number of those who are out there will be better, worse or different for anything these lives had spent themselves to gain and to give.

If such thoughts came to me, as to any one they might, must they not have come often and often to those of whom I have been telling? and must not these men have been seized at times with a wistful sense of the humor of their situation? If so, what gave them courage to keep on and to endure until the end? Was it that by some fatality they were bond-slaves to the remote, from whose dom-

the prophets of that mediation which will make labor and delight one thing? May it not be possible for us after their leading so to live and strive in the moment that more and more of the whole toward which it tends may be felt in it? And this whole, the while, will it not come so to be conceived that its real presence in the crumb of bread and drop of wine may make of our daily partaking a sacrament as bright as it is enduring?

If so, and, as it seems to me, only if so, will these thinkers about the whole have found that for which they seemed to waste their being — the response of the man living the moment, which is everyman. Then will we the studious have brought back from our wanderings with these " souls of men outworn " something more than ineffable things and memories of dreams dreamt with them. To men bound for the most part to live the moment, that moment would not have lost its throbbing intimacy because it had lost its solitude.

Now of all desirable things, one may feel and in a poor fashion of words try to tell how desirable they are, without having much hope of securing them for himself or of being able to offer them to others. But it cannot be a bad way to begin winning something for oneself at least by enriching one's reflection with all the stored experience of history.

RETROSPECT AND PROSPECT

And as history is not always easy to gather, it is at least a generous impulse to tell of what is to be found there a little more simply and compendiously than others have cared to tell it. Which done — and the doing of it has that peculiar quality of giving to the labor of the moment its sense of participation — it is time to look about one with one's own eyes.

What under such circumstances the private eye, turning from the past and peering into the future, thinks it sees there, might well be kept private for all the authority it can have and for all the interest it may have for another. Each will have his own vision of the horizon. But it has never been found that the truth is in the end better made out by each holding his own counsel as to what he timidly thinks he descries there. No, out of the confusion of many witnesses comes what little we have guessed or can hope to guess of truth, and no less of that truth which, because it deals with the tie that binds the least with the greatest of things, I venture to call religious.

In these pages, little or no mention has been made of those great historic religions in whose name temples and cathedrals have been built, and throngs have been moved to worship and to war. This neg-

And even among those who did not mean to be critics, we find some devoutly maintaining that divine revelation brings naught that reason and experience cannot confirm; naught, then, they could not have reached: " Non alia est philosophia, i.e., sapientiae studium, et alia religio," writes John Scotus in the ninth century. " Quid est aliud de philosophia tractare nisi verae religionis regulas exponere? Conficitur inde veram esse philosophiam veram religionem conversimque veram religionem esse veram philosophiam. (*De praedest. proem.*)

But those who from revelation turn to *reason* and those who turn to *experience* for evidence in all matters, are of two different tempers of mind and habits of thought. The first we found represented in Spinoza with his *Ethica ordine geometrico demonstrata;* the second in Hume with his methods of natural history and human history.

Of these two schools, I think we may regard the first as definitely closed. That is, to establish the existence of God by logic alone and as a necessity of thought, would only be dreamed of today by those who meant by God, by logic, and by thought's necessity something quite different from anything the seventeenth century rationalist could have meant by those terms.

Yet to say that the *method* of a Spinoza is dead,

is not to say that his contribution to the spiritual problems with which he dealt is naught. Nothing could be more important to our whole attitude toward these problems than Spinoza's insight: The scientific demand that we treat nature as an inviolable mechanism and the ethical demand that the human element in nature remain a free agent *are consistent*. It can readily be seen that all the rest of one's thoughts about the world must hang upon one's acceptance or non-acceptance of this reconciliation of mechanical necessity and living freedom. (It must not be supposed, however, that all later thought was agreed that Spinoza had effected this reconciliation; perhaps the present writer is without company in thinking that Spinoza's indications in this sense may be followed to a clear and satisfactory issue.)

If the method of rationalism has lost meaning for us, do we then abide in the confidence that experimental science must find all that is to be found of an object for religion to attach itself to? To my thinking, no! Or rather, the meaning of experience and with it of empirical science has been so altered by later reflection that the relation between human desire and human finding is no longer conceived to be that austere separation which a Hume, a Clifford or a Huxley made the basis of intellectual honesty and even of moral honor.

There is nevertheless one result of the empirical philosophy which it is hard to believe we shall ever set aside. Whatever we may have come to think experience means, those who have once entered into the spirit of these clear thinkers will not lightly abandon the idea that *experience is one*. There is not for most of us one kind of experience that confirms the law of falling stones and revolving planets, another unrelated kind that gives us a sympathetic but inarticulate insight into life and its ways, and yet another which in incomparable theophanies reveals to us another world. In a word, empiricism has taught us to accept the postulate that whatever the nature of our beliefs, their meaning must be communicable, their evidence must be demonstrable by one to another.

What has happened to change things since Hume's day is, first of all, just a deeper searching into the meaning of experience itself, with perhaps this finding: that the reality our empirical science reveals to us is not merely a thing found and received but also *a thing willed and made*. Kantian criticism it was that suggested the part played by the knower in the formation of the thing known. This knower was not merely informed by experience as to the world he had chanced on, but of himself he informed his world. Imperfect, disconnected and unconvincing as were Kant's efforts to state and illustrate this conception, it is nevertheless to him that one turns for the first suggestion of that idealism whose more recent expressions have been illustrated in the chapter on Pragmatism.

Meanwhile, really unaffected by this development of method are Schopenhauer's gloomy findings and Nietzsche's exaltation of the might of man. Just as the facts of life as he observed it left Hume unable to point to anything in experience that could guide life religiously, so these facts as Schopenhauer more fully took them in left life irreligious and blind. Again, it was but what he took to be a broader experience that led Nietzsche to conceive the destiny and perfectability of life to lie within the control of life itself, and it is only a still broader view of experience that robs this philosophy for us of what inspiration it had and leaves it but a gospel of gritting-the-teeth.

Yet we may not lay aside these two " findings " regarding life without noting how deeply each has seen into the human heart. If the insight of each is directly contradictory to the insight of the other, it is because the human heart is in contradiction with itself.

RETROSPECT AND PROSPECT

It can listen, this heart of man, to the voice of Schopenhauer crying for peace. It can understand this voice even to the point of feeling that the peace of those who have ceased to be is happier than the being of those who have lost hope of peace. Not indeed for us is the " melius est ipsum esse quam non esse " of older simpler times.

But on the other hand, Nietzsche would not make the appeal he does if man did not shrink from every vision of peace that has ever been offered to him, as from something worse than nonentity. Indeed we " envy not the dead that rest. . . .

> What peace could ever be to me
> The joy that strives with strife? "

Thus it would seem that the philosophy which alone can bring to pass that gladness of the moment which comes not from its content, but from what there is mixed in it of fulfilment and of promise — that philosophy must give validity to two theses:

(1) Reality must in all its aspects be shown to be such a thing as human effort may make and mould.

(2) This effort must set before itself an ideal in which are consistently included all that is genuine in the old ideals calling themselves Peace and War.

RETROSPECT AND PROSPECT

If the first of these theses was the topic of the chapter on Pragmatism, the second was that which inspired the conception of Progress. Only if to each moment of life there is vividly present the sense that it is a moment of creation, and equally present a satisfaction in the vision of what is to be created, can the moment be a joyous one. Not joyous in a way to wring from us a " Verweile doch! du bist so schön! " But joyous with that quality which would let our *Ave* be a welcome to the hoped for, our *Vale* a benediction on a promise left behind.

If our Modern Thinkers have done aught to help us so to pass a moment, why, so, let them pass.

FINIS

INDEX

317

INDEX

318

INDEX

INDEX

320

INDEX

conditional good, 268–273; as viewed by reformed morality and by amorality, 273–276; and conflicting ideals of peace and war, 277; final definition of, 277–281.

Providence, Hume on "Particular," 112–115.

purpose, consistent with mechanism, 53–55, 84–92.

quakerism, German, 146.

Rabelais, 153.

rationalism, of Descartes, 41–45, 104.

realism, 218; in science, 221; in history, 222–226; in ethics, 227; in religion, 228, 240–242; in art, 228, 229.

religion, "Natural History of," 110; Kant's attitude toward, 131; identified with philosophy, 310.

Rousseau, 258.

Royce, 157, 267, 285, 287, 289, 293.

Schelling, 149, 159.

Scherer, on Amiel, 217.

Schopenhauer, iv, 154; "World as Will," 158–161; on universal strife, 162–167; forerunners, 167, 168; followers, 168, 169; on suicide, 169, 170; on the beautiful, 170–172; on civil law, 172–173; on moral intuition, 173–175; on denial of will, 175–178; on Nirvana, 178–181; and Nietzsche, 186–193; 313, 314.

Schopp, letter describing Bruno's trial and execution, 31–34.

Spinoza, iv; family, life, death, 39; and Bruno, 39, 40; and Descartes, 40–46; on popular theology, 46–51; *ein Gottrunkener*, 52; purpose and freedom, 53–55; knowledge, goodness, happiness, 55–63; 104, 187, 310, 311.

suicide, Schopenhauer on, 169–170.

superman, iv, 195, 196, 205, 208.

super-superman, iv, 208.

sympathy, Hume on, 126; Schopenhauer on, 173–175; Nietzsche on, see pity.

Tasso, 259, 263.

teleology, see purpose.

Tennant, 300.

tragedy, Schopenhauer's con-

INDEX